THE WOMEN WE WATCHED

....

A CELEBRATION OF MOTHERS BY THE SONS AND DAUGHTERS THEY NURTURED

Charlene Keys-Bowen & Friends

The Women We Watched - Charlene Keys-Bowen. -- First Edition
Paperback ISBN 978-1717201331

Also available in eBook and Hardcover formats.

E-Book ISBN - ISBN: 978-1-7322664-0-7

Hardback ISBN - ISBN 978-1-7322664-1-4

This book is dedicated to the women we watched:

Earthel, Sandra, Winford, Precious, Diane, Jennifer, Fannie, Rose Mary, Ollie, Ethel Lee, Ella B., Mertis Jean, Bettye, Wilhelmina, Catherine R., Ruby, Margaret, Catherine S., and Barbara Jean

May your beauty, love, courage, faith, and integrity inspire and compel for generations to come.

ACKNOWLEDGEMENTS

Thank you to the incredible men and women who contributed to this project, sharing rich stories of the women they watched. I am forever grateful that you accepted the invitation to take this journey with me. Thank you for your generous spirit and for your support of the mission. You helped make it all possible.

Contributing Authors

Cynthia Alexander, Nicholeen Brame, Ben Brezeale, Tonja Brown, Tara Edwards, Kemberly Harrington, Marcel Henry, Tina Hodges, Sonja Jackson, Chris Leevy Johnson, Elonda Neal, Janice Roberts, Tracey Steele, Reggie Tuggle, Evette Tuggle-Beckett, Valarie Perkins, Michelle Vereen, and Tigerron Wells.

To my wonderful husband, Don and my incredible son, Chris I could not have embarked upon this project without your encouragement, love, and support. You both make me better and I love you.

To Dominique (Brian), Megan (Donnell), and Diana (Steve)... I celebrate you as mothers and I am confident that you will be the women your children watch.

To my father, Charles Huiett Sr. and to my mother Earthel Jamison Huiett, posthumously, thank you for teaching me to live with grace and peace, for supporting my dreams and for being amazing parents!

To my village - Alice Blakely, Virginia Coffield, Georjean Simmons, Karen Williams, Willie Herriott, Martha Smith, and Rose Bailey -Thank you for your nurturing friendship, love, and prayers. You helped me grow.

CONTENTS

The Women We Watched

FOREWORD

It comes as no surprise that what started as an idea for an acceptance speech delivered by the principal author of this book, my wife Charlene Keys Bowen, has culminated into an amazing collection of short stories that I hope will both inspire and instruct readers for decades to come.

My wife came home from work one night and over dinner, while sitting on the barstools surrounding the island in our kitchen, she shared with me a task she needed to complete by the next morning. She had been selected by Women in Cable Telecommunications (WICT) as one of their 2017 Women to Watch and had learned that day her acceptance speech needed to be scripted in advance and was due the following morning. She said to me, "I'm not sure what I want to say."

I immediately said by way of suggestion, "Why don't you write about your mother as she was the woman you watched and by whom you were so deeply influenced?" Charlene immediately embraced the idea.

Several weeks later on September 25, 2017 at the Marriott Marquis Hotel in New York City, Charlene, along with approximately a half-dozen other women, accepted awards in various categories from WICT. I asked her prior to the event if she would be able to get through her speech without getting emotional. Come game time, she delivered a heartfelt speech with tremendous poise and humility. I, on the other hand, was crying like a baby, overcome with emotion and pride not just for Charlene, but also for her touching tribute to the woman I have come to know very well, albeit largely through stories.

By the time I met Charlene's mom her health was deteriorating. As a result, I never had the good fortune of really knowing on a personal level the remarkable woman Charlene talks about so often. Almost daily, in the two and a half years since her mother's passing, Charlene comments on how much she misses her mom or refers to her mother in some other way. She is present in many ways; often Charlene reflects on something her mother said, or what her mother would have done if she were encountering whatever given situation we are facing.

The lessons Charlene learned are evident and abundant and the special bond she shared with her mother is so apparent. As I have listened to the many stories Charlene has shared with me about her mother, it is crystal clear they were like "two peas in a pod;" very similar people born at different points in time. Both women are highly intelligent, resourceful, caring, giving individuals with boundless energy who give far more to others than they ever needed and accepted in return. Strong women of faith, their belief in GOD was and is the source of their strength. Earthel could have been Charlene or perhaps said differently and more appropriately, Charlene is Earthel.

Because so many people were touched by Charlene's remarks at the WICT Awards ceremony, she was inspired to expound upon her speech and to invite a collection of friends and colleagues to write about the women they watched. I know how touching Charlene's tribute to her mother is and this book is full of stories of many other mothers that I am sure will move and touch readers in profound ways as well.

Like Charlene, the authors profess deep love, admiration, and gratitude for "the women they watched." Common themes like humble beginnings, overcoming obstacles, hard work, faith, and perseverance help meld these individual stories and these diverse women together in a way that aptly defines the power of mothers.

It is always a pleasure to recommend a good book to others. It is an even greater pleasure when the primary author of that book is someone you know, admire, respect and love!

While we're recognizing mothers, I would be remiss if I did not recognize my own mother, Gladys Bowen who is now deceased and to whom I owe a tremendous debt of gratitude. While she was not my biological mother, she was the only mother I have ever known and I loved her deeply. Abandoned on the sixth stoop of a boarding house at the corner of Massachusetts and Pacific Avenues in the Inlet section of Atlantic City, New Jersey as a newborn, I owe everything to my mother who took me from the foster care system and provided me with a foundation of unconditional love that is still with me today. To my mother, I could do no wrong and while we did not have much in the way of material possessions, there was nothing she would not do for me as she was one of the most giving and caring people I have ever known. I never heard her say a mean thing or do a bad deed to any other human being. I never saw her take a short cut for personal gain, and she had no vices; she didn't smoke, drink, gamble, lie, cheat, or steal. Heck, I never even heard her say a curse word, and believe me, I gave her many reasons to swear while I was growing up! My ability to love myself and love and trust others is largely the result of the deep and never-ending love she gave to me, especially during my formative years. It is largely because of her that I am a caring and good-hearted person and not full of bitterness and distrust like so many other children who were abandoned.

There is one more important thing, which I believe the readers of this book need to know: For all the adulation and respect Charlene has for her mother, there is one other subject about which Charlene is equally passionate and which she talks about almost as often: DreamBee Foundation, which Charlene created as a means to prevent and eliminate child abuse. All of the costs of producing and marketing this book have been paid for by Charlene personally and one hundred percent of the proceeds from this book will go to further the charitable work of DreamBee Foundation.

The power and impact of a mother's love defies natural laws and explanation. In this book, the authors shared their most personal and intimate stories, their attempts to describe and celebrate the women who most shaped their lives. In recognition of the importance of mothers, Rudyard Kipling once said, "God could not be everywhere, and therefore he made mothers." In a similar and more contemporary vein, Stevie Wonder had this to say about his mother: "Mama was my greatest teacher, a teacher of compassion, love and fearlessness. If love is sweet as a flower, then my mother is that sweet flower of love."

Reading this book will surely touch you in special ways, perhaps some happy and some sad. It may even make you a better and more loving person and we definitely need more of those people in our world today. There is an old adage that says, "They don't make them the way they used to." That adage would certainly ring true for the women you will come to know in this book. It is my sincere hope this book will inspire mothers – especially young mothers and mothers to be, to love, inspire, and empower their children so that one day their children will celebrate them and prove this adage incorrect.

Don Bowen
April 5, 2018

INTRODUCTION

On September 25, 2017, I was honored to receive the Woman to Watch Award from Women in Cable Telecommunications (WICT) upon the recommendation of the company I work for Charter Communication, Inc.

As I thoughtfully considered what I would say during my acceptance speech, my husband posed the question to me "Wasn't your mother the woman you watched?"

Inspired by his question, I decided that my speech would be about my mother and that I would dedicate the award to her memory.

The audience's response to the speech was overwhelming, and I was encouraged to publish the speech.

The feedback inspired me to write more about why my mother was the woman I watched, and I was also moved to invite a talented team of contributing authors to write about the women they watched.

This book is a compilation of those stories. I sincerely hope that you will be inspired and informed by the protagonists in these stories.

The Women We Watched

EARTHEL JAMISON HUIETT

By: Charlene Keys Bowen

My Mother was not only the woman I watched, she was also the woman I adored. My observations of her colored the blueprint for my life, and informed me of how I would live my life and how I would raise my son.

Standing 5'4" tall with skin color that resembled a beautifully ripe peach; mom was loving, intellectually gifted, authentically compassionate, and extraordinarily resilient. Mom valued education, was an avid reader, an incredible cook, and she loved celebrating family and close friends. I got to know her keenly sharp wit in her later years, and I cherish my memories of her wonderful sense of humor. She lived her life with passion and freedom, and I believe that her profound trust and belief in GOD allowed her to do so. I am, and forever will be grateful that she was the chosen vessel through whom I would enter this world, and the person to whom I would look to for counsel and perspective throughout my life.

Mom had effortless beauty. She could go without makeup and look absolutely polished. I loved shopping for her. She maintained a proportionate figure throughout her life, and she would beam whenever I, or my sisters would arrive with shopping bags. Prior to leaving for church on Sundays in outfits that seemed to always highlight her best qualities, Mom would apply a small amount of press powder with a red sponge, a slight swipe of nude or lightly cinnamon colored lipstick and a dash of lightly floral cologne. She would emerge from her dressing room smiling and occasionally she would imitate the half turns of a runway model. As the compliments rang out, she would burst out in laughter and say as only she could, "Thank you darling."

My mother was a fount of wisdom, whose spirit, which I believe was born out of an unending belief in a true and living GOD, powered me. Her encouragement made me believe that anything was possible, and that I could accomplish anything I worked hard to achieve. It was her faith that compelled my desire to have a personal relationship with GOD. She is the one person who has had the greatest influence in my life, and I am confident that my relationship with my mother was as GOD intended. That is, until I was confident enough to know that as a result of my personal relationship with Christ, I would receive unmerited love, grace, and guidance from the Holy Spirit, and until I was able to stand in the truth of my creator, and know that I know, that HE was and is the source of all that I am, the person through whom I entered this world, my mom, would stand in the gap and provide me with unmerited love, grace, and sound guidance.

Throughout my life, I observed my Mom as she skillfully navigated the highs and lows of life. She had a remarkable ability to efficiently put things into perspective, and an enormous capacity to forgive. Her life, in sickness and in health, served as a navigation system for me, a sort of North Star; helping me to plot the course of my life as I navigated life's twists and turns. Because my mother modeled standing in your truth, I am able to stand in my truth, and to be unabashedly guided by the spirit placed in me by my creator, even in times of disappointment and uncertainty.

My mother's wisdom was rooted in Judeo Christian principals, and for me, her assessments of people and situations were, for the most part, spot on. It's amazing to me that irrespective of the location or circumstance, I generally go to a place in my mind that offers perspective on what my Mom might have said or done. As a young adult I wore an armband that was branded WWJD; which stood for 'What

Would Jesus Do?' The acronym was symbolic of a movement begun by Christians in the 1990s as a reminder of their belief in a moral imperative, which was to act in a way that demonstrated the love of **Jesus** through their actions. Just as I wondered WWJD, I also have wondered WWMD; 'What Would Mom Do?'

Mom was the oldest of ten children, born in 1936, in Columbia, South Carolina to Nathaniel "Pat" Jamison, a tall handsome laborer, and Leatha Benjamin Jamison, a beautiful, pearl wearing housekeeper. I never knew my grandparents; they were deceased before my birth, but based on the joyful expressions and affectionate stories my mother shared about them both, I am certain I would have absolutely adored them. Mom also spoke very lovingly of extended family; telling demonstratively humorous stories about them and the people she grew up with. A picture of my grandmother hung prominently in our living room, and from time to time I would see my mother just stare at the portrait; during happy occasions she would do so with a smile, and during sad occasions, with tears in her eyes. I now understand how important that picture was to Mom; how much strength she must have drawn from just having that familiar smile close by. I keep a picture of my mom on my desk and several on my smartphone for immediate access.

Mom lost her father at the age of 11, and her mother at the age of 20, both to catastrophic illnesses. Her relatives, mostly cousins, stayed close to her after her parents were gone. Her cousins always referred to her as good looking and smart. And no matter what circumstance these cousins found themselves in, I only remember Mom always being kind and loving to them. The only time she would be firm with them was if they said something inappropriate in front of her children or younger siblings. She fiercely protected our innocence and when I became a mother, I did the same with my son.

I remember my Mom's cousin, Christine, who was known to occasionally take extra privilege with adult infusions. Christine would stop by on Friday evenings so that her "pretty cousin," her affection-ate referral to my mom, could make sure she was stunning before she set out for a night on the town. I was very young, around 7 or 8 years old, but I recall the girlfriend-like laughter that surrounded their conversations. Soon after Christine arrived, Mom would quickly style Christine's hair, freshen her up with a little face powder, and finish her off with a light dab of her perfume. It was like magic. Mom would transform her look, and Christine would literally scream and say, "Ah, Cousin you make me look so pretty!" The two of them were about as different as night and day, but there was a familiar love that transcended their notable differences. I watched my mom as she dem-onstrated how to love unconditionally.

Comparatively speaking, our life journeys have been quite differ-ent, and I am confident that my journey would not have been as richly rewarding had it not been for the prayers, love, guidance, and sacrifice of the woman I watched, my mom; Earthel Jamison Huiett.

Characteristic of time and place, mom grew up poor. When shar-ing her stories of lack and limits, she would say to me, "Baby we were so poor," then she would shake her head, laugh, and say, "Lord Jesus" with a hand wave and a slight nod of her head. She'd go on to describe the time when she had to wear kitten heals without stockings.

It was the winter of 1961 in Columbia, SC. Snow and freezing rains dominated the forecast, but my parents could not afford to take the day off. The hope was that Dad's baby blue Star Chief Pontiac could make it up the hill on Rosewood Drive, which was about two miles from their home in Columbia so that Mom could to get within walk-ing distance of her job. Mom said she had planned to hop out of the car near her work and walk briskly to avoid too much exposure to the frigidly cold weather; an unusual condition even in the peak of winter for the midlands of South Carolina.

The kitten heels she wore that day were the only shoes she had suitable for work and she needed to get to work to earn money to help care for her sisters and brothers now that her mother was deceased. Sadly, the car could not crest the hill mostly because of the condition of the tires. Mom said she did not have a choice so she got out of the car, braved the snow, freezing rain, and bone chilling temperatures, and walked the remaining few blocks of her journey. As I listened to her tell this story, it only reinforced what I had thought of her life: my Mom's dedication was unwavering, her sacrifices too numerous to count, and as a very young woman, her struggles were far too many. Together we found laughter in this otherwise sad story, mostly because I generally wear heels without pantyhose. In part because it's fashionable, in some ways because it's rebellious, and for me, it's economically sensible because I usually find a way to rip them badly within the first hour of having them on. I eventually convinced Mom to only wear pantyhose when she really dressed up. She had beautifully bronze-colored, shapely legs and she really didn't need to wear those overrated nylon contraptions. This is small in scope, but a wonderful reflection of the love and trust we shared.

My maternal grandmother's death, a year after the birth of her youngest child, left a tremendous void in the lives of her children and it ushered in a new narrative for my mother's life. And, though their father, my mother's stepfather, was still alive, and lived several decades longer, he left the burden of caring for all seven of his children to his stepdaughter, my mother.

Sadly, I was given insight into the enormous burden my mother felt as she relived this painful period during the final days of her life. In the Intensive Care Unit at Palmetto Baptist Hospital, I stood at my Mom's bedside holding her hand. The room was very cold and Mom had been taken off a ventilator only a short while earlier. In a semi-conscious state Mom painfully uttered a heartbreaking plea to her mother, begging her not to die. Tearfully, she murmured "Momma what am I going to do?" Visibly panicked, she asked about her four-year-old sister and one-year-old brother. "Please momma," she said, "don't leave me, I can't do this by myself."

I had observed my mother cope with grief and loss before, but watching as she unknowingly revealed this intense vulnerability and fear was unlike anything I'd ever witnessed. My heart ached for my mom. I longed to protect her and to become the mother, the guardian, the confidant, and the friend she had lost as a result of her mother's death. I stood at my mother's bedside; my fingers intertwined with hers, deeply saddened and extraordinarily strengthened all at the same time. Tears streamed down my face as I pondered how my mom had made it. How had she overcome this epic amount of grief? I wondered how she had found the courage to fulfill this massive role in the lives of her younger siblings. How did she, at such a young age, become the family's matriarch; nurturing, encouraging, guiding, disciplining, finding good in everyone and everything? Where did she get the strength? How did she hold it together? And then I remembered her source of peace. The source she prayed that all of her children would find; the one source she insisted we cling to. A peace came over me and I realized that I was cut from the same cloth as my mother. I saw my own vulnerability, and I recognized the source of my strength.

My mom was always a fierce protector of her family. Once while visiting my aunt, I got into a fight with some of her neighbors. I stood about 4'6" tall and weighed about 65 lbs. soaking wet. I remember being pushed and shoved; occasionally I made contact with my loosely structured swings. If you knew anything about me, you knew that I preferred reading a book to protecting myself against three angry little girls, and you also knew that I was not an accomplished fighter, so I was not in any way enjoying the experience. Suddenly, I felt a force grab me. It was so powerful that it sent my body spinning through the air causing the fabric from my blouse to separate. Fear consumed me when I realized that the force propelling me was the little girls' mother, Mrs. Jenkins. Once freed from that traumatic situation, I made my way back to my aunt's house, just as my mom was driving up. Upon seeing me, she immediately asked what had happened to my blouse. Tearfully, I began to recount this horrific event that still pains me as I write about it today. My mom placed her purse on my aunt's kitchen table, walked out the back door with me in tow, and headed for those kids' house. Mom knocked on the door, and when it was answered, she did not pause for greeting or introduction. My mother reached back and pulled me beside her and calmly asked Mrs. Jenkins why she had placed her hands on her child. It was visibly clear that my mom was not happy, and all I remember was Mrs. Jenkins saying, "Mrs. Huiett, I am very sorry about this and I will pay for your daughter's blouse." My mother's only response was, "If you ever touch my child again, it will be your last time."

Now, I realize that a lot could have been interpreted from my mother's statement, but Mrs. Jenkins did not ask for clarification, nor did she challenge my mother's statement. She was clear. My mom's behavior left an indelible impression on me. She showed me how to draw a hard line in the sand when it came to defending those you love and want to protect. I knew that when I became a parent, if compelled, I would do the same.

There is another occasion I recall when my Mom stood up for me. It was a beautiful Sunday afternoon in early August; I guess I was about 14-years-old and I was sitting on our front porch reading. A young woman who looked about 25-years-old was walking up our street and decided to stop in front of our house and began shouting insults and obscenities. The more I ignored this woman the louder she became. Having overheard the noise, my mother walked calmly onto our front porch. Even with Mom present, the lady continued her rant. My mother asked her what was the problem and her response was something indecipherable, or grossly inappropriate. I remember Mom saying to her, "You will need to move from in front of my home with this noise." I started to get a little nervous because this lady seemed out of control, and my Dad was at church that evening and Mom and I were home alone. The lady continued with her ranting, which quickly turned into threats.

Having heard all that she could stand, and without hesitation, my Mom reached into her pocket and retrieved Betsy, the .22 caliber pistol that her uncle had given her shortly after her parents died. She held the gun down by her side and said, "This is my last time telling you to move from in front of my house with this disrespect and to leave me and my child alone." With the same rambling tone, only this time it was apologetic, the lady began to move at a rather rapid pace away from our home. My mother warned her that if she returned, she would be forced to shoot her.

I was in awe of my mother. She would later say to me, "Sometimes, baby you have to show people better than you can tell them." This became a defining moment for me. My sweet momma had the audacity to stand in defense of her home and her child. Her actions liberated me. Because of my mother, I embraced courage and fearlessness at a very young age.

My mother wanted everyone to do well and to have a great life. She was selfless in many ways and she was not a complainer. She was not a weak person, and she did not tolerate foolishness. She honored her body and she made her home a safe clean place of refuge for her husband, her children, and her sisters and brothers. One of my lifelong friends reminded me of one my mother's selfless acts of generosity. She said, "When your mom gave you guys money to take to school for snacks, she also gave me and my sisters money." What was so incredibly moving about her comment was that she made this statement at my mother's wake. She went on to say, "Your mom not only wanted her children to do well, she also wanted and encouraged other children to do well." What a compliment. I am grateful for my mother.

My mother married the love of her life, my father, a handsome young man from Georgia whom she loved and honored until her death at the age of 78 in 2015. They were a handsome couple and they were completely committed to each other. It gave me great joy to hear my Dad refer to Mom as Honey or Sugar. Almost sixty years into their marriage, and with a twinkle in her eyes, Mom would smile and say Dad was her best friend and her boyfriend. They shared everything. Their years together included the best of times and the worst of times, but the lovely banter between the two of them always ended with them saying that they loved each other. They never left the house without kissing each other.

My father credits my mother with having the business sense in their marriage. Early on, they had very little money and both worked outside the home to put food on the table not only for my older sisters and brothers, but also for my mom's sisters and brothers. Like most young couples, they were renters until one day they received word that the house that they were renting needed to be vacated because the owner's family member had lost his home and needed to move back into the family house. Shocked by the news and uncertain of where they would move, Mom decided that she did not want this to ever happen to her again so she convinced my Dad that they should purchase the house that was going into foreclosure. My dad, understanding that they were certifiably, with a capital C, broke, replied that there was no way in the world they could afford to buy that house. They did not even have a down payment. He was not making a lot of money and the best they could do was to find another place to rent, keep the lights on, and keep food on the table.

According to my dad, Mom had a different idea. She believed if she shared her story with the owner, and if they committed to making payments on time and honored that commitment, they would be granted the loan. Mom and Dad agreed on what they would make as an offer on the house, and how the two of them working together could accomplish their goal of home ownership. Within a few days, the two of them were seated before the attorney who owned the property, tendering an offer on the foreclosed home. Dad always says, "I don't know how we did it." The attorney asked if we could pay $500 more, and he and mom agreed that they could. My parents owned the house in full by the time they were 28-years-old. A drunken driver killed one of my older brothers, who was only four-years-old at the time, and my mother insisted that the insurance settlement received from his death be used to pay off the mortgage on the house. That house at 1653 Andrews Road remains the family home today. I have often wondered about my impenetrable can do attitude. I now have great clarity, as Dad has recited this story to me over the years, from whom I inherited it. It was my mother; the woman I watched.

When I was in elementary school, my Dad began doing janitorial work at night in addition to his day job. He and mom quickly grew this side hustle into a thriving business boasting clients like Merrill Lynch, John Hancock, Siebels and Bruce, Motor Credit, Cummins Engines, Wometco, and a string of law firms too numerous to name. My mother was an equal partner in this venture and she worked equally as hard. Their profits from the business far outpaced their salaries from their day jobs, but they held onto those jobs to secure health insurance for their children. Dad was thrilled that we had officially moved into the Black middle class so he convinced my mom to look at homes in the newer neighborhoods around town; the kind where up and coming families of color were moving to, but my mother would always compare the quality of construction, the hardwood floors, crown molding, and the solid wood doors found in our circa 1950 home to those houses and you can guess which one eventually landed on top. As an adult, I asked my mom why she was so resistant to moving and she shared with me that they owned our home free and clear, and that it was paid for with money gained from the death of my brother. She'd then go on to say, "I just don't want to go back into debt." Tears would well up in her eyes as she moved around the kitchen. It was clear to me that it was not as simple as crown molding and wood doors; and although I too am a big fan of the older homes, I think for Mom, as long as she was in that house, she somehow felt like my brother, Mike, was also there with us. I concluded that she didn't want to leave because she did not want to leave him. She was devoted to her child, even in his death.

Turning twenty for most young people is usually a time of celebration with rites of passage into adulthood and the freedom to pursue their dreams. Most twenty-year-olds live a relatively carefree life and are not expected to assume the role of a more tenured adult. This was not the case for my mother. Shortly after my mom turned twenty, her mother passed and her stepfather deferred all matters relating to the upbringing of her younger siblings to her. There was no middle ground. It was either she takes care of them or they go into group homes.

My granddad, the only living grandfather I ever knew, was an elegantly tall, dark, and handsome man, with blue eyes and silky silver gray hair. I always loved when he came to have coffee with Mom and Dad on Saturday mornings. The older kids would be watching *Soul Train* or *American Bandstand*, and I would be seated near one of the interior kitchen doors reading or writing as Granddad shared with my parents his embellished accounts of his life on the railroad as a porter. Those stories, the smell of freshly brewed coffee, the delectable scent of pepper-cured bacon and buttered toast, and my parents laughing at Mr. Allan, as my Mom referred to him, warms my heart to this day, and gave me great insight into my mother's heart. Mom modeled treating people better than they deserve. This life lesson has been one of the most important lessons I have ever learned, and quite frankly one of the most rewarding.

Granddad endearingly referred to my Mom as Ess, and though her stories of him as a stepfather were not flattering, as he got older, mom's concern for his health and living conditions resulted in she and my dad moving him from down in the "Bottoms" near Arthur

Town where he lived, to a home closer to where I grew up. Granddad bragged to all of his friends that Ess was moving him on up. He was very proud; Mom was giving him a better life and he wanted everyone to know. My grandfather later died in that house, but before he died, he said to my mom with tears in his eyes, "I'll die a happy man because my daughter moved me up out of them Bottoms." This move for Granddad elevated his stature in life.   Because of it, he would say to us, "Oh, I'm somebody," and with a twinkle in his blue eyes, he would start to chuckle. I watched my Mom show compassion and respect for the person most responsible for her having to defer her dreams. No finer example of compassion and respect could she show to someone who had shown so little compassion and respect for her.

After my grandmother's death, her friends and confidants became my mother's friends and confidants, and though none of mom's aunts stepped up to assist her with the EPIC responsibility of raising her siblings, her uncle rose to the occasion as only he could. This tall, athletically built, no nonsense man would enter our home with a booming voice and a brilliant smile. He was larger than life, and he adored his brother's only daughter, my mother. He would visit on Friday or Saturday, usually in the evenings, and I loved hearing the laughter that would resonate from our kitchen when he was sharing his larger-than-life stories about his adventures on the railroad and throughout the community. He always urged my mom to take care of herself. "You are too young to have so much responsibility, gal," he would say, then he'd nod his head for Mom to walk him to the door where he would always place some money in her hand; usually $100 or more.

My uncle was not an educated man and he was very proud of the fact that my mom was smart and in his words, "knew how to take care of business." Mom would help him manage his personal affairs in a thoughtful and confidential manner. He was a very proud man, and he appreciated Mom's respect and discretion. Whenever she would read correspondence to him, he would say, "Look at your momma, now you've got to grow up to be smart like that." My response was always, "Yes sir." It pretty much guaranteed me a quarter, and on good days, a dollar.

Mom's behavior demonstrated to me the requirement of treating people with respect and the undeniable necessity of allowing them to maintain their dignity.

Mom honored her mother's memory by living her life as an example for her brothers and sisters. She insisted that they be educated at least through high school and she did everything she could to encourage them to become productive members of society.

I loved watching my mom interact with my sisters and brothers. She always brought out the best in each of them and she nurtured all of us as only a loving and devoted mother could. Mom believed that if we had healthy self-esteem, we would be able to weather the storms of life. She did not promote arrogance or elitism; she promoted each of us having a good sense of who we were, what our strengths were, whose we were - children of the most high GOD, and why we were here - to do as much good as we could until GOD called us home. She would say to each of us, "Always hold your head up, respect yourself, and don't tolerate disrespect from others." She insisted that we be independent and educated. I recall my mother having a wonderful relationship with my big brother. As a mother, I turned to my mother's playbook when it came to raising my son. It facilitated the very special relationship that he and I share today.

As a young adult, whenever my big brother came home, he would greet Mom with a big hug and kiss, followed by loads of compliments on her undeniable, unchanging beauty, her magical abilities in the kitchen, and her warm and loving spirit. He adored Mom and she him. His untimely death was very difficult for my mother and I watched her health go into rapid decline after his burial at the age of 29. I had graduated from college and was off on my journey, but I knew Mom was really sad, so I began calling her every day just to check in to make sure she was okay. My daily calls also provided her with reassurance that I was okay. I spent a big portion of my earnings as a young adult paying for long distance telephone calls. I had always felt a need to make sure Mom knew how much I loved her and how much I wanted her to get better. She appreciated my calls and she said she looked forward to them. We became each other's confidant and that lasted until her death. I should note that although she is no longer with me physically, I still share my deepest thoughts with her and I feel strongly that she is with me.

Mom had a special way of connecting to each of her children as only a mother could, and she and I connected through our love of learning. We were both early risers and when it was just the two of us, talking, preparing meals, or just waiting for the other family members to wake up, Mom nurtured and encourage my curiosity, my love of reading and writing, my sense of self-worth, and my belief that I could accomplish anything I set my mind to. She taught me how to be the best person I could be by demonstrating authenticity and compassion. On the weekends she would reach out to our older neighbors to make sure they were okay, dispatching her children to rake a yard, run an errand, or just visit with them for a brief period. She would share what we had in our cabinets and freezers with families who were less fortunate, and still find time to get us all ready for church on Sunday. She would do all of this and she would never complain. I remember asking once, "Mom, why don't their families help them?" and she would say, "Baby, all we can do is the best we can. Don't worry about why others won't do, just do what you know to do is right." This advice along with treating people better than they deserved to be treated taught me emotional intelligence and gave me a blueprint for how I would live my life.

When Nikki Haley, now US Ambassador to the United Nations became the 116th Governor of the state of South Carolina, my mother called me and said, "Charlene, I'd like for you to consider politics.

I think you should run for Governor of South Carolina. You would be so good for this state." This was not in any way a slight to former Governor Haley; my Mother was actually very proud of her; she just believed enough in whatever it was that she saw in me to encourage me to take on a broader leadership role. Couple President Obama's election with Governor Haley's election, and Mom said she thought the time had come and when people got to know me and began to understand the type of leader I would be for the state, she was sure that I would win the gubernatorial race. She would go on to say, "I'm so proud of our Mayor, that Steve," referring to Columbia, South Carolina's mayor, the Honorable, Stephen K. Benjamin, "and that baby from Morehouse," referring to former SC State Representative Bakari Sellers. "I want you to help this state. I may be dead and gone," she said, "but I know you will do something big to make a difference in this world." Spoken only as an adoring mother could, I responded to her by saying, "Thank you, Mom for believing in me." She ended our conversation by saying, "What can I help you do to get started?" Mom was a no-nonsense person and she was committed to helping me live up to my highest potential.

When I was eight-years-old, my dad was doing some electrical work in our home. He was not a certified electrician; nor was he a certified plumber, carpenter, roofer, or landscaper, but he generally performed those duties at our house. Mom became increasingly concerned about the electrical sparks that continued to fly as Dad tested his ability to repair an electrical device, but my dad's only response was, "I know what I'm doing." Hoping to protect me, the only kid not outside running around, from a possible electrical mishap, Mom said to me, "Let's go outside and plant some flower seeds." Because I was always happy to do things with my mother, I put down the book I was reading and ran outside to help Mom plant some flowers.

Our front yard was always well-maintained and included green shrubs and beautiful red, knockout rose bushes. Mom's plan was to plant pink and white flowers to compliment the landscape of a yard that seemed so much bigger then than it does now. As we planted the seeds, Mom looked over to me and said with a look of intentionality, "If your daddy isn't careful, he is going to blow this house up. I have to protect you, you see, because you are very smart and I am going to teach you how to take care of business so that you will be able to handle things when I am gone." Maybe my mom was concerned that she would leave this earth at a fairly young age like her mother and she did not want to leave her youngest daughter without depositing what she believed were essential wisdoms for not just surviving, but also for thriving. Also, knowing mom, I somehow believe that she said something equally as profound to all of her children.

Mom could not have done more for my life. She believed in me and she thought that at a young age I had promise. Over the course of my life, I watched how people reacted to and interacted with my mother. Her graceful presence commanded respect. She was not argumentative or combative, but she would speak logically, factually, and without apology. She was not a formal neighborhood leader, but her opinion was always sought and she understood the big picture. Whenever someone spoke negatively, she would respond in a kind and respectful manner; "Well that's just one man's opinion, and he has a right to that. Don't own it, take from it what you can, but don't let it stop you," she would say. I have often gravitated to those words and have shared them with mentees and colleagues. I think Mom was saying, "Be informed by the commentary, take from it what is edifying, but don't allow it to cripple you."

Growing up, I stayed close to my amazing mother. I wanted to learn from her as much as I could. Her educational opportunities were cut short, but her love of reading and learning and her enormous faith in GOD gave her a wealth of knowledge and wisdom. While sitting in the lecture halls of the Harvard Business School in Boston, Massachusetts, I fought back tears, knowing that my mother's health was in decline and wondering what her life would have been had she been afforded the opportunity to sit in those very lecture halls.

Given the opportunity, I think my Mom could have been an effective and influential corporate or political leader. She understood people well and she genuinely wanted the best for all mankind. She was smart and she was not afraid to call BS, BS. She practiced systems thinking, not ever knowing that how she naturally thought had been studied and implemented by brilliant thinkers and practitioners globally. Mom often spoke about the role of government in our society and how it could be leveraged for good. Mom did not lack substance, she embraced integrity, did not shy away from hard work, made more sacrifices than she should have had to, and was keenly aware of the growing disparities throughout our society; especially as it pertained to children and the elderly.

Mom instilled in me a fierce love of reading and learning. She modeled, brilliantly, the importance of running your own race. She did not concern herself with what others had or were doing, and I never witnessed my mother comparing herself to anyone else. She was authentic and she was consistent. I have had an abundance of peace in my life because of these behaviors I observed of my mother and I have been purposeful to model them for my son.

My mother's youngest grandson, my son, once described her as the most courageous person he had ever met. In a third grade homework assignment, he wrote, "My Grandma is not afraid of anything; she is my hero." No truer statement could be made of my mother's attempt to secure a job in the tall office building on Main Street doing office work at a time when her African American contemporaries were getting jobs as housekeepers.

According to mom, circa 1966, she saw a Help Wanted ad in The State newspaper for office help in one of the big office buildings downtown on Main Street. From mom's perspective, this was perfect. She had always planned to work on Main Street and her time had come. She told me that she shared with my dad that she was more than qualified for the position, and that she was going to go downtown and apply. She fluctuated between moments of sadness and comedic relief when she retold the story of her visit. She said when she arrived, there were two white women who asked if they could help her. Mom replied that there was a sign in the window and a newspaper ad that stated they were looking for office help. She said she immediately felt the unease of the two women. In the spirit of the *Little Engine that Could* by Watty Piper, Mom went on to say, "I'd like to apply for the job." Mom told about how the two women looked in disbelief at this courageous or crazy woman of color standing before them and sharply said, "Honey, there is no opening here." Mom understood what happening, but decided to ask a few questions. She asked why the Help Wanted sign was still in the window and why the ad was still in the newspaper. The women had no answer, and they asked Mom to leave. Mom would laugh every time she told the story, and although she did not get the job, I got a valuable lesson from her experience and I admired her courage and tenacity.

Mom was particularly funny and she loved a good laugh. During a hospital stay a year before she passed away; she told one of the visiting church officials that she had instructed me to bury her in a place of perpetual care and to select a spot not terribly far from the primary road that ran perpendicular to the cemetery. She said to him, "Joe, make sure you don't let things get out of control at the church." She went on to say, "My final resting place will face the road you drive home on, and if you let things get out of control, I might throw a rock and hit your car." He shared that story as he spoke at my mother's funeral on October 18, 2015.

I watched my mother throughout our time together on earth. In May 2004, I returned to my hometown of Columbia, South Carolina. My new role as Vice President and General Manager for one of the Fortune 500 Companies in the city made my parents and especially my mother very proud. With the exception of business travel and or vacations with my son, I saw my mother every day for eleven years. What a blessing, and I count it all as joy!

Mom loved seeing her youngest grandchild almost daily and the two of them developed an incredibly special relationship. While he was in middle school, she would say to him, "Now I expect you to go to college, and you can count on me being at your graduation." In May of 2013, my mother wept as she witnessed her youngest grandchild, Christopher, graduate from Morehouse College and she watched in awe as the 44th President of the United States, Barack H. Obama delivered the commencement address.

She would often say to me, "Baby, I don't want you to be by yourself." I had been divorced for 17 years so she was thrilled to witness Don Bowen's proposal of marriage to me in her living room just before noon on March 12, 2014. Mom was so happy for me that she insisted that we immediately go shopping for my wedding gown. Her health was on the decline and though she was not able to attend my wedding ceremony, she had given us her blessings and was there with us in spirit.

On Wednesday, October 14, 2015 I arrived at my mother's hospital room around 1:30 pm. She wore a hospital gown and a black satin bonnet. The sound of the CPAP machine was loud and her breathing was labored. My mother's doctor grabbed me as I entered the room and with tears streaming down her face, she said what I had known my entire life: "Your mother is such a beautiful person." She went on to say that she and Mom had sang songs together, and that Mom had given her advice on raising a happy family. She tearfully made reference to my mom's beauty; "She is so pretty." It's ironic; there I stood comforting this physician as she tearfully shared her thoughts about my mother, knowing that Mom was in the final hours of her life.

A couple of hours after I arrived at the hospital, the hospital Chaplain stopped by my mother's room, introduced himself, and asked if he could pray with us. With great dignity, my mother introduced herself, explained that she was hard of hearing, and then introduced me. She said, "If you are here to pray, we would appreciate that." She smiled warmly, accepted the offer of his hand, and clasped my hand tightly.

Mom had shared with me that previous Saturday just before I called the ambulance to transport her to the hospital that she would not be coming back to that house; the one at 1653 Andrews Road that she had owned since the age of 28, and had convinced my dad, when they were certifiably broke, that they could afford. She said, "Baby, I'm going to my other home now." I sat at my mother's bedside and watched over her until she departed this life at 6:45 am on Thursday, October 15, 2015.

This was the most difficult and yet the most peaceful experience I've ever had. It was difficult because I knew I would miss seeing my mother's beautiful smile and miss receiving her warm hugs and kisses. I would miss her energy, her enthusiasm, her laughter, and zest for life. I would miss the woman I had watched my entire life, the woman whose opinion of me meant the most, who always loved me unconditionally, and who invested the most in me. It was peaceful because in the silence of her hospital room, occupied by just the two of us; no crash carts, hospital staff, or blinking lights, GOD gently received my mother into His kingdom.

Before Mom died, she whispered to me, "You've been a good daughter to me, baby; the best," she said, "and if I know anything, I know that you love me." Those affirming words will sustain me until I transition from this earth to my heavenly home. My only hope is that I will do for my son what my mother did for me.

Earthel Jamison Huiett
(1936-2015)

The Women We Watched

FANNIE L. MURPH

By: Valarie Perkins

Our mother, Fannie Lee Murph, personifies fortitude and dignity. I watched her navigate life's highs and lows with pride and grace and create a fulfilling life for herself and her family. Her resilience and strength inspired us all to want to live up to our potential and encourage others to do the same.

Although she initially only completed school through tenth grade, she understood the importance of education and encouraged her children and others in our neighborhood to be lifelong learners. When she pushed us all to go to college or pursue a trade, she led by example by getting her GED when she was in her late 40s. She then went farther and gained her cosmetology license and her Commercial Drivers License (CDL) so she could start three separate successful businesses that she maintained well into her 70s.

This level of success may not have been expected from a woman who had lost both of her parents by the age of 13. When her mother died from an unknown illness and her father was later murdered, our mother was raised by her widowed and childless aunt. Her early life experiences shaped her into the independent woman we love and respect.

Mom taught us about the important things in life. We learned independence and how to care for our families and ourselves. She taught us decency and that we are all worthy of honor and respect. She showed us how to love big without fear. And we learned the importance of community and giving to help others. Although our mother was never short on words to share with anyone, she taught her strongest lessons through her actions.

This is a collection of stories about a few of the values our mother instilled in us.

A wise person once said that we become who we are out of the necessity of what life demands of us. This is most evident in Mom who is an ever-living example of what a strong woman should be in a very complicated world that places value on a person's race, gender, and income.

Mom worked for a small vending company in the early 1980s. The work was quite labor intensive and the supervisors were very oppressive in their management style. Needless to say, Mom endured as much as she could for the sake of the family, but she began to reach her breaking point.

She was never afraid to speak her mind. Obviously, this kind of personality in an oppressive environment was a problem waiting to happen. After deciding she would no longer hide her disapproval, the company's leadership terminated her employment and asked her to vacate the premises.

When she left, our Mom said she would never work for another person again, and we saw how this experience encouraged her to become an entrepreneur. We watched her grow from someone with no formal education into a successful businesswoman. Not only did she earn her cosmetology license, but she also had our father build her a salon, and she negotiated a contract with the local nursing home to style the residents' hair. Not satisfied with that success, she also opened a ladies clothing store downtown. She eventually obtained a CLD license so she could become a school bus driver during her down time.

As her grandchildren say, she was definitely a hustler. Her entrepreneurial spirit has spread throughout our family. All three of her children and two of her grandchildren have been or are currently entrepreneurs.

Mom has a special relationship with her grandchildren, especially her only grandson, Theo. When he was in elementary school, she took the time to teach him about entrepreneurship. When his sister attended a weeklong summer camp about entrepreneurship, Theo felt left out because he was too young to attend. Mom, however, made sure he wouldn't be left out for long and he learned about entrepreneurship from her firsthand.

As Theo spent his days with his grandmother, she showed him how she purchased clothing for her store and sold them to her customers. During this time, he also learned the difference between wholesale and retail prices. As Theo learned more about running a business, he wanted to put these lessons into practice.

While at the local flea market one day that week, Theo asked Mom if he could use his allowance to purchase some toys and candy to sell to the students at his sister's camp. Mom was thrilled and proud to help him launch his first business. He then persuaded the camp director and his sister to allow him to sell his products to the other camp participants.

Theo made more money than any of the official camp participants that summer! His grandmother was so proud of him. He recognized that he learned the fundamentals of entrepreneurship directly from his grandmother and he has since applied these skills to other ventures and they have helped make him a strong, independent person.

Mom also taught us that we are worthy of decency and respect. We learned this as a result one of her many shopping experiences.

One fall day, she was shopping at a local store and fell in love with some apple trees on display. She was excited about her purchase and looked forward to the future harvest so she could share her apples with her family and friends. In the first year, the tree grew but didn't produce the large apples the store had promised. Although she was disappointed, she decided to wait another year in hopes for more.

Over the course of the next year, we watched her continue to nurture and care for the tree. The following harvest season, she was again disappointed when the tree didn't produce the apples she had hoped for. She started to suspect that she had been deceived and did not receive the product she had paid for.

After another year and similar results, Mom became really upset. She felt she had been used and taken advantage of. Although she did not pay much for the tree, she knew the store should have been honest with her and treated her with the same respect as any other person, no matter her race, gender, or income level. When she visited the store to share her concerns, the staff laughed at and dismissed her. A sarcastic manager eventually told her that they could not do anything without seeing the tree.

We assumed this was the end of the story, but we should have known better: (Our Mom doesn't back down from a challenge!) She convinced my father to use a tractor and chain to dig up the tree, and she returned to the store to get her refund from a three-year-old purchase.

Although we jokingly retell this story among our family, Mom was teaching us about self-respect and that we all deserve honesty and to be treated with dignity. We also learned to speak up for ourselves and that sometimes our actions will speak more than our words. Because of the way our Mom approached this issue, we learned that you must always do your part. If things do not go as planned, then when you finally do speak up, you can be certain you did all you could.

Independence

Mom managed the household finances per Dad's request. Even without a formal education, she made sure they purchased a home and invested in savings bonds and rental properties. She refused to use credit cards or finance companies and encouraged us to pay cash when possible. She knew the importance of being able to manage money and taught her children how to do so.

When I, the middle child and oldest daughter, graduated from college and started my first full-time job, Mom told me that I had to pay rent to continue staying in their home. I thought it was the worst thing they could have done to their child. Mom explained, however, that I was making more money than both of my parents and I needed to know how to manage my money because I would never be able to live anywhere free of charge.

I reluctantly paid our parents rent each month. However, I was pleasantly surprised, when I learned that my parents were saving the money and gave it to me when I moved into my own apartment. Because of their actions, I was able to start my adult life with substantial savings and learned how to manage money so I could take care of myself and later help my family.

Jennifer is the baby of the family. On her 15th birthday, she didn't wake up to the traditional birthday song like most people, but instead to a unique gift from our Mom. In her typical direct fashion, Mom said, "Happy Birthday. Here's your card. Now get up because you have an interview at Winn Dixie grocery store."

Jennifer wasn't only surprised because she hadn't applied for a job, but there was nothing in the card. She soon learned that Mom got the interview for her so could "get her own money." Thankfully, Jennifer got the job and learned the importance of being able to make her own money so she would not have to rely solely on others.

A week after her high school graduation, Jennifer totaled the car that she had been allowed to drive. Mom told Jennifer that she would help her get a new new car, but that Jennifer would be responsible for payments. Jennifer, unwisely, thought Mom was joking. When they went to the Toyota dealership, she was still convinced our parents would purchase her dream car. She soon discovered that our Mom meant exactly what she said.

During this time, Mom taught her to hold onto all payroll checks for her records so she could average her salary and would know how to negotiate a price based on her income. However, both of our parents went into the bank without her, and our Mom came out after a while to ask if she felt comfortable making an $89 monthly car payment. Simply put, Mom chose the car and negotiated a reasonable payment amount for her.

Once they returned home, our Mom told Jennifer that our parents would only give her one payment, one tax payment, and one insurance payment toward her car. When she turned 18, Mom put the car in Jennifer's name, and she received her own payment coupon book. After having the car for 10 years, Mom bought it from her as a spare vehicle. That experience taught Jennifer how to navigate a large purchase and how to value her personal items.

Love

Our parents have been married for sixty years and Mom has genuinely loved and respected our father throughout their marriage. She has encouraged her daughters, Jennifer and I, to do the same for our husbands, especially if they are good men. Even though she was never a stay at home wife or mother, she always made sure that our father was well fed and taken care of after working a long day.

Only a few days after I got married, Mom tried to convince me that I should also cook daily for my husband. However, I am not the type of woman who will spend hours in the kitchen to serve and please a man. One morning my Mom called me to tell me that I should prepare a big breakfast including grits, eggs, and bacon for my husband that day and every morning afterward. Needless to say, I didn't take that very well but tried to do as she said. Now nearly 32 years later, my husband is still talking about that memorable morning, saying I definitely cooked as I was told, but forcefully slid it to him with the eggs and bacon clinging to the side of the plate.

Although Mom and I sometimes have different ideas of how to love our husbands, she has shown us the importance of never taking your spouses for granted and continually showing that you love and care for them.

Jennifer and her husband have been married for 20 years. They dated for a year while she was in college and for an additional four years after she graduated. By today's standards, most people would say that they knew each other very well and were ready for the next step. Once he proposed, they decided to move into the home they would eventually share as husband and wife.

Our Mom, a traditionalist, believed that unmarried couples should not live together, regardless of whether or not they were engaged. Instead of addressing Jennifer when she shared her plans, Mom waited until she was perming Jennifer's hair. As Mom moved the chemical through Jennifer's hair, she lectured her about how "shackin' up" wasn't the right thing to do. Jennifer jokingly remembers being told off while sitting in the beauty chair. Unfortunately, she wasn't able to walk away because if she had and the perm wasn't complete, she ran the risk of losing all her hair. Well played, Mom!

During that conversation, Mom also shared some other marriage advice, which she had also shared with me. Some of her nuggets of wisdom are:

- When you get married, spend time with other married couples that have good relationships.
- Keep your single girlfriends out of your house.
- Don't go to bed mad.
- Cook for your husband. (Jennifer took this advice. I am still struggling with it!)

Jennifer admits she was glad that she stayed in the chair and listened to our Mom's advice. (Besides, she tried other stylists, and they just couldn't quite straighten her hair the way our Mom did!).

In addition to loving her spouse, our Mom also showed her love for her family by being a listening ear and offering spiritual advice based on GOD's word. Ebony is Mom's first grandchild, and they have a very special bond. When she was in her mid-20s, Ebony was experiencing what she calls her quarter-life crisis. Because of various experiences, she began to question her faith.

One morning she was overwhelmed and reached out to our Mom in tears before six am. She said she knew that our Mom would be the perfect person for her to talk to at that moment because she needed the warmth and comfort with which Mom showers her grandchildren.

During their talk, Mom prayed with Ebony and referred her to Psalm 56, a chapter she values still today. Ebony admits that although she is still weary of the "extremely" religious, she admires Mom's faith and ability to really trust in GOD the way she does.

Our Mom has a genuine spiritual connection and relationship with GOD. We have listened to her call each of her family members' names in her prayers throughout the day and each night. Because of this, we know her love for her family is not only earthly, but also spiritual. We have witnessed her relationship with and love for GOD. This is something we all continue to try to replicate for ourselves.

We smile at the many memories Mom has given us. Recalling and discussing these stories and the lessons learned with my family has been wonderful and therapeutic but also bittersweet. It only has been a few months since Mom had a stroke and was diagnosed with dementia. As a result, we are learning that because of it she cannot always remember these memories and enjoy them with us any longer. Regardless, as we continue to care for and love her as the disease progresses, we will reflect on these stories and continue to thank her while we can for all she has done for us.

As the descendants of my mom, Fannie Lee Murph, we are all proud to continue to share with others her legacy and values of love, independence, dignity, and community.

Fannie L. Murph

The Women We Watched

BARBARA JEAN HENRY

By: Marcel Henry

As I think about my mother and how she influenced my life, I reflect on how the ideals, habits, and practices of her daily life have become the fabric of my own. Growing up, I tried to reject the ways of my parents as I sought to become "my own man." Today, I embrace every habit, mood, characteristic, and idiosyncrasy that reminds me of the first woman I ever loved.

My earliest memories of my mother began at about age four. We lived in a fourplex apartment complex in Berkeley, California. I remember walks to the corner store owned by the Lee's and my mother's lessons on how to say "please" and "thank you." While those sound like small things that every child learns from his or her mother, I am reminded of my mother's kindness and grace.

I walked to that same store alone for the first time before I started kindergarten. My mother walked me to the corner and repeated to me the rules she taught me about crossing the street. As she stood on the corner, I made that one block trip by myself, turning around every dozen steps or so to wave and make sure she was still there. Mr. Lee knew me well and I was able to hand him the note listing the item she sent me to the store to buy.

She was right there waiting for me when I walked out of the store and I couldn't wait to give her the paper bag and tell her that I did it all by myself! While it's hard to imagine anyone letting a four-year-old out of their sight in today's society, it was the earliest lesson I can remember from my mother; one that helped me to become independent.

My parents were 19 when they married in 1962, and I was born later that year. As a child, I never thought of my parents as young parents - just as my mama and daddy. But as an adult, I grew to appreciate the effort it took to stay together as a young couple and all that my mother did to provide me with the foundation that set the course for the rest of my life. A cornerstone of that foundation was education. With my mother's guidance, I learned to read before my first day of school, and my mother ensured that I took advantage of every educational opportunity available, which would serve me well later in life.

I learned the importance of advocacy in education by watching how my mother advocated for me. The late 60s marked an interesting period in the life of our country, and Berkeley was not immune to the challenges of a segregated society. Berkeley voluntarily desegregated its school system in 1968 and I had an opportunity to attend one of the best schools in the city. That same opportunity led to me being selected for Berkeley's High Potential Program which exposed me to a learning environment not available to all students. This included a experimental reading comprehension program that taught first graders to read using the phonetic alphabet. This precursor to Hooked on Phonics involved me bringing home schoolwork where I spelled the word cat as "kæt" or root beer, as "rœt beer." Although my mother was not a trained educator, she took the opportunity to learn this method of teaching along with me so that she could continue to help me with my schoolwork. As a result of her involvement and care for my education, I was a very advanced reader, with a vocabulary several years above grade level. She kept a few of those workbooks locked away as a keepsake well into my adulthood. My mother's advocacy for my education instilled in me the desire to do the same for my own children. My daughter jokingly recalls me reading the *Wall Street Journal* with her as a young child, helping her with the pronunciation of business and financial terms while sipping on a juice box.

I didn't realize how much of a Superwoman my mother was while I was growing up, but it now seems as if she took care of most everything in the household in addition to keeping a job. In the early years, I remember her taking a seasonal job at the Dole processing plant during peach season. We had peaches every day during that time and my grandmother would make the world's best peach cobbler using the fresh fruit my mom would bring home during the canning season.

During the 70s she became part of Americana when she worked in one of the iconic Fotomat photo booths. She would dress in her uniform, a red and yellow smock and beret and people would drive up to one of the gold-colored pyramid roofs to drop off their Kodak film for developing. As a kid, I thought that was the coolest job and I recall the days of riding with Dad to pick her up from work. She kept that job until she was robbed at gunpoint and no longer felt safe.

Her move to Pay 'n Save as a retail clerk resulted in my first unofficial job. Neighborhood shoppers would take the shopping carts home, creating a shortage of shopping carts in the store. The summer before I entered the sixth grade, I started roaming the neighborhood surrounding the store, collecting shopping carts for $0.75 each. That kept me busy during the summer and taught me the value of work. I'm pretty sure that money supported my comic book and model car collections. Pay 'n Save closed at some point, but I recall the close bond my mother built with her co-workers, some of whom remained friends for many years to come.

After the store closed, she moved on to the Caterpillar Tractor plant where my father was working. Unlike the other places she worked, I couldn't visit the plant, but I knew she worked hard, transitioning through all three shifts over the course of her employment. The life lesson I learned from watching my mother work was the value of hard work. Both of my parents did what was required to take care of me and my sister. As I look back, I know for a fact that we were always her number one concern.

Through the hard work and determination of my parents, we moved from apartment living to our first home in Berkeley and later to a beautiful home in the Oakland hills. Throughout all of the changes, my mother always managed our household with style and grace. My parents were married for 54 years until my mother's death in 2015. Although my father was always there, I went to my mother first for comfort, advice, and guidance. She was always the one I felt that I could talk to.

As a young adult, my mother gave me the space I needed to grow into the man I am today. If I didn't call as often as she'd like, she'd jokingly call me Bryant Gumbel, a reference to a *Sports Illustrated* article that said that Bryant was not nice to his mother. I'd call my mother to get cooking advice, as I was determined to learn to cook for myself. While living at home, I'd stand in the kitchen talking to my mother while she cooked. I remember calling her while attempting to cook rice for the first time so that I could make sure I added the right amount of water to the pot.

My mother deferred to my grandmother for the cooking during the holidays. My grandmother was a fantastic cook and the holiday meals were always a feast. It was always interesting to see the dynamic between my mother and her own mother. You always see your own mother as one of the heads of the household, yet her deference to my grandmother (on most things), helped me learn respect for our elders and an appreciation for the wisdom they bring. When it came to my uncles, that was another thing altogether! My mother stood 5'2" on a good day, but that did not stop her from putting her brothers in check if she felt they were being disrespectful to my grandmother or if they'd been drinking too much. As quiet and mild-mannered as she was in most cases, she had no problem taking control of the situation.

My mother was not a religious person, meaning that she was not a regular church-goer. She always made it possible for my sister and I to attend church with other family members, and later in life, she would attend church with my sister or the members of her social club, The Ebonaires. This aspect of my mother provided me with one of my greatest life lessons - the distinction between a good person and a religious one. My mother was one of the most genuinely good-hearted people I've ever known, though she was not religious.

My mother was a beautiful woman, but never flaunted her beauty. She dressed modestly, but was always dressed! There would never be an occasion where she left the house without her hair done and maybe a touch of lipstick. I don't think I ever heard her utter a curse word, but she was never afraid to speak her mind. She gave up smoking in the 60s when she became pregnant and would treat herself to a glass of wine on special occasions. She was always kind and was never known to gossip or have an unkind word to say about anyone. I found that these traits became important to me as I began to develop my own relationships later in life.

My parents moved to metro Atlanta from Oakland in 2000. My grandmother remained in the Bay Area, and my mother continued to care for her from across the country, managing her finances, arranging for grocery delivery and medical appointments. Her vacation time would be spent taking trips back home to look after my grandmother in person. She did this even though she had two brothers living in California. She was the caretaker and had assumed the role of the matriarch of our family. From this experience, I learned about the changing roles in our family dynamics through this cycle of life. This was probably the first time I saw my mother exhibit real stress. My grandmother wanted to live an independent life, and despite the efforts of my mother, my sister, and I, she refused to leave her home in California. Yet, through it all, my mother remained steadfast in her devotion and obligation to care for my grandmother.

As a child, my worldview of my mother was just that – of a mother. She and my father were my parents, and my relationship with them was based on that experience. As an adult, I was able also to see her as a wife, and like any other interpersonal relationship, a marriage requires management. In many ways, my parents' marriage was a traditional one. They married at 19 and started a family soon thereafter. My parents went right into the workforce, and as a result of hard work, they provided our family with upward mobility and provided a great life for my sister and me. While the dynamic between my parents was somewhat traditional, I sometimes wondered how they managed to stay married for a lifetime. They were in many cases polar opposites of one another. My mother was mild-mannered and my father could be boisterous and bombastic at times. It wasn't until I became a married man myself that I saw the magic in their relationship. My mother kept my father grounded, a source of reason when emotion might otherwise prevail. They were "old school" and were truly inseparable. My mother loved my father unconditionally, and even through some of the toughest times that a marriage could endure, she was there. Not because she was dependent on him, but because she loved my father with all of her heart and saw marriage as a real commitment for better or worse. I know beyond a doubt that my father loved my mother with all of his heart. Their marriage helped define what I wanted my own marriage to be like one day. My mother also provided the blueprint for many of the qualities I would eventually find in my own wife.

I married in 1987 and my mother instantly became the world's best mother-in-law. My wife and mother got along quite well and my mother was never one to meddle in our marriage or offer unsolicited advice. The same grace she'd shown throughout her life was the same grace extended to the family I had started. To our son and daughter and my sister's two boys, she was Yaya, and there was nothing that made her happier than being a grandmother. She even added a personalized plate to her car that said YAYABOB, Yaya, for grandmother and Bob, my father's nickname for Barbara.

The year 2009 marked a sad turning point for our family. Mom was diagnosed with breast cancer. While we were optimistic about her prognosis, we knew that things would have to change. I could see the effect the diagnosis was having on my father. His usual effervescence was more subdued and while he said that everything was going to be just fine, his demeanor could not hide his concern. Mom on the other hand, continued to operate as though it were business as usual basis with little to no change in her daily routine. It wasn't until she had to undergo chemotherapy and radiation that the ravages of cancer begin to show. Mom was a licensed hairdresser and could use marcel irons like no one I've ever seen. She did her own hair every morning before leaving the bedroom, let alone the house, so the loss of her hair was a particularly painful part of the treatment process. After finding a wig that she liked, she went back to work showing a type of inner strength I am not sure that I could muster under the circumstances. She also continued to take care of my grandmother, putting her own illness aside to care for her. It was her way of managing cancer instead of letting it manage her.

She managed her treatments well and got a clean bill of health not long after. We were overjoyed at the news and mom went back to a full time work schedule and daily routine. She was especially happy to be able to attend the graduation of her granddaughter from Howard University in 2010. During this time, I saw my mother exhibit strength not only for her own sake, but for the sake of my father as well. Over the years, their routine seemed to bring them even closer together. My father, who runs his own insurance business, would stop work each day to pick my mother up from work. It's not that she didn't have a driver's license or couldn't drive herself, it just became part of their routine. Throughout her treatment, she was determined to keep as much of their normal routine in place as possible. I know that she did this more for him than for herself. Even in the midst of her own challenges, she still managed to put others first.

Unfortunately, the cancer returned in the fall of 2012 and had metastasized to other parts of her body. This time treatment was more aggressive and it took its toll. Initially, she did not tell my grandmother about the return of the cancer in order to keep from worrying her. My sister lived nearby and stepped in to help manage some household details. Throughout all of the challenges my mother faced, she continued to try and do her hair and makeup every morning and take walks with my dad while she could. Her zest for life, even in the most challenging of times, was inspiring. I would ask her how she was feeling and the answer was almost always, "I'm doing okay." Many of us have had lives touched by cancer in some way, but it is nothing short of amazing to witness the bravery of those in the midst of their battle.

We continued our family tradition of cake and ice cream and an off-key rendition of "Happy Birthday" for my mother's 70th birthday in September of 2013. The picture of her blowing out the candles on her cake is one of my favorite images of her. I look into her eyes in that photograph and I see sheer joy. She was surrounded by the people that mattered most to her. Her family was there and that is what brought her the most pleasure.

The following year was very difficult as mom's condition began to worsen. As with many cancer patients, the treatment sometimes felt worse than the disease. This was the case for my mother. The days following chemo were unpleasant, yet she still tried to do everything she could to maintain her routine for as long as possible. Not only was it a pick-me-up for herself, but I knew that once again, she tried to give my father hope all the way up to the time when she could no longer care for herself.

When we moved Mom to hospice, my sister and I made sure that she was never alone. My fear of losing her was only overcome by my desire for her to no longer be in pain. It was during our time alone, in that room, that I was able to hold her hand again, just as I had when I was a child and tell her how much I loved her and appreciate all that she did to make me the man that I am today.

The woman I watched was a woman of beauty, grace, and dignity her entire life. I can now see that I am truly molded in her likeness, character, and temperament. From her, I learned how to be level-headed and calm even in stressful situations. I learned the importance of education and instilled those same values in my own children. I learned that our greatest joys come not from material possessions, but from being surrounded by the family and friends that mean the most to us. If I had one wish for every family, it would be for them to have a mother like mine.

Barbara Jean Henry
(1943-2015)

The Women We Watched

SANDRA CLARDY BREAZEALE

By: Ben Breazeale

My mother would say her life began when she was six-years-old. Born in 1944 in Greenville, SC, she came home to a small house shared with a 17-year-old father, an 18-year-old mother, two grandparents, and a great-grandfather.

But it was 1950 at the Piedmont Pentecostal Holiness church, where six-year-old Sandra Clardy walked down the aisle and started life on her own. That night, the minister explained that sinners were like bugs hiding in the dark. When the light of salvation was revealed, they scattered to hide from judgment. But some also were attracted to the light. She was so attracted.

The means were modest. Her father had dropped out of school in the eighth grade, but knew how to hustle and worked hard to make money. His early experience with bootleg rum runners gave him the opportunity to become a founding driver of a dirt track race experience, known today as NASCAR, being created by Bill France, where he could sometimes pick up $10 on weekends. My mother was loved, but never treated as a child. From the beginning she was an equal to the adults. Instead of bedtime, she went cruising in the car every night with her teenage parents who made a pallet in the backseat for her to sleep on while they drove.

"Sandra, how can you stand to go all day without brushing your teeth?" her mother once asked her when she was in kindergarten. That was the first time her mother had ever mentioned the concept. Her parents were honest kids, but there was no instruction, no guidance.

The Holy Spirit became her guide. Eternity became her timeline. And the church became her structure and her hope. She held onto the thought that everyone was equal in God's eyes.

These are the lessons she was desperate to convey each night before I said my prayers and every morning before I started my day. To me, she was lovely and she was magic. I shared with her my feelings and ideas about the world and she really listened, like I was a kindergarten equal, as she had been. She captured the concerns of my little life and somehow had daily direct conversations with the Almighty on my behalf.

Two things drove her parenting: her lack of guidance as a child, and her deep love for God. Consequently she never let a day slip. Encouraging, teaching, telling, warning. Days were like the flowers of the field, here today and gone tomorrow, and there were many things she felt responsible for imparting. She explained to our family that we had been brought together and divinely placed. We were to recognize the mystery and the responsibility of our mission each day; to generously reach out to all we encountered, wherever God placed us, and to share with them the hope within us. She was intense but more than that, she was intentional.

She hadn't had this direction as a child, but there had been helpers. Sunday school teachers, kind aunts, and her beloved live-in granddaddy "Fern," who would tote her around anywhere and everywhere he went to the relief of her young parents. She was a talented singer and was Granddaddy Fern's pride. Even as a child, the church had her singing solos at the Sunday service. Fern would drive her around to music halls and other churches on the weekends to showcase her young talent to anyone who would listen. It gave her confidence. It solved some of the mystery of her divine purpose. She was given the gift of song as a light to those around her. She shared with them her story and her hope.

Music became her escape and her platform. At 14, she got her driver's license and was then truly in charge of her own affairs. Both her mother and her grandmother had decayed into a semi-drugged and depressed stupor. She now cooked for the home and attended all parent/teacher conferences for her younger brother, Jim. She performed in high school musicals and traveled to area churches and gave speeches, her "testimony" of how God had helped her.

During her junior year a kind teacher nominated her for Girl's State, an American legion leadership program made famous by a picture of a young Bill Clinton attending Boys Nation and shaking hands with John F. Kennedy. She was accepted and quickly elected as one of two delegates to represent South Carolina at Girl's Nation – the national group. She traveled to Washington D.C. and was subsequently elected to serve as the president of Girl's Nation. This was one of the highlights of her life.

The official picture of Mom with Kennedy is a treasured family heirloom. Even Clinton only met Kennedy as part of a large group. Official presidential minutes and pictures from a Google search record the Oval Office meeting on August 3, 1962 of Sandra Clardy, president of Girl's Nation, with the thirty-fifth president of the United States. The impact on my mother was a deep and direct confirmation of her mission. Only God, designing a specific plan, could have taken a poor 17-year-old girl from South Carolina into the Oval Office for a formal meeting with the President of the United States. From this meeting onward, the intensity and boldness of her personality blossomed. "Go big or go home" became a theme of her storytelling and her life.

I now understand the excitement, authenticity, and the drama she imparted in her bedtime Bible stories of David and Goliath, Noah, Samson, and the twelve disciples with access to the God who created the universe. My mother described to me the poor, lonely shepherd

David being escorted into the courts of King Saul. Like her, he had also been plucked from obscurity and was similarly escorted into the most powerful halls on the earth. It was amazing to listen and impossible to doubt a word of any story she told. She taught me how to engage my imagination and to communicate to others with energy and purpose.

Her platform secured, Mom attended the University of South Carolina as a freshman with measurable experience and accomplishment. She continued her singing and her speaking, but to a larger audience and with more courage and intensity. She found kindred connections with students in South Carolina who joined in civil rights marches and protests of the era, going against the prevailing sentiment at the time of many beloved South Carolina churches. To her, civil rights were an extension of her deeply held conviction that all were equal in God's eyes; equally loved and equally in need.

Upon graduation, she married my father, an excellent man who was soon to become an Air Force officer, which would ensure their travel around the country and the world over the next twenty-five years. He was from a traditional stable family, one built on generations of parents committed to each other, and to being parents and raising children. Part of her attraction to him was that she yearned to have this example as a part of the legacy for her own children. Once again, every decision was intentional and had an eternal purpose.

In 1970 she had twins, my sister and I, and found herself stationed in Rapid City, South Dakota, where the bedtime prayers and Bible stories commenced in earnest. She put us to bed on time, taught us to brush our teeth, and was driven to ensure that no needed instruction or important life lesson would be neglected or omitted from us. She continued her speaking and her singing and was an admired leader among the Midwest Christian churches we traveled to as she told her story. In time, we became part of the lore. She had prayed for twins and received direct confirmation it would come to pass. This became another example of the connection between the tangible world and her mysterious world of faith.

These connections to the unseen world, like her prayers, were never ceasing. My childhood is awash with examples of chance meetings and near misses, orchestrated by angels in service of specific plans, somehow all working together for the common good. She planted this faith deeply in my life and the lives of those around us, changing many lives for the better.

On one occasion my parents were short on money. We had taken a family trip to Denver and on the way back, we would be short of funds for anything other than gas and car cushion change for small drive-through meals. At a city gas station, my parents bumped into a woman who had been to one of my mother's concerts and heard her speak. She had been greatly affected by my mother's words and had made positive changes. The woman's husband was the managing director of a big restaurant in the city. Two hours later we were at his restaurant thanking him for the free meal for the family. My mother took the time to teach us the context and blessing in each and every one of these encounters.

As I recall growing up my mother's consistency stands out. The bedrock principles never shifted. Here was a pilgrim travelling through this world with a story to tell and a duty to fulfill. She radiated love and relished new challenges but found it all but impossible to be frivolous or light-hearted. In her mind, people needed to be connected, encouraged, or woken up as the limited days continued to march towards eternity.

She stayed committed to education, eventually earning a doctorate and two master's degrees over the next 25 years – despite frequent moves. During these years, we lived in South Dakota, Virginia, Washington D.C., Belgium, and South Carolina – a product of the Air Force life. Moving was stressful. But because of mom, every new setting became an opportunity to discover a fresh chapter in the mission. She encouraged my sister and me to reach out to people and to discover the surprises God had in store at each new place. Her perspective kept us safe and turned our fears into an adventure. What could have depressed us gave us confidence and excitement. This is one of the lessons for which I am most grateful today.

My high school friends were drawn to her light. Today these 50-year-old men still ask about her and convey the impact she had on their lives. It was uncommon to find someone with such conviction of purpose who really cared about each person around her. Teenagers recognized this instantly and she never turned any of them away. During these years, she would make a school lunch for me each day. Included with each lunch every morning was an index card with an encouraging quote from the Bible. A few inquiring friends noticed and began asking her if she would make a card for them each day. By tenth grade, my mom was a one-woman Hallmark factory, writing out special daily cards for dozens of teenagers.

In my senior year of high school I met my future wife, Ally. My mom fell in love with her instantly. Upon meeting my in-laws for the first time, mom shocked them by commenting on the potential of our future marriage. Over the next five years, during the ups and downs of college dating, she never lost faith in what she felt would be the perfect partnership for her son. Her special insight was proven again when Ally and I married when I graduated from college. Mom placed Ally's wedding portrait in the honored central staircase of her home, right next to her own wedding portrait, and that of my twin sister, Barb.

She has never stopped giving to her children. Mom gave generously to all she encountered, but we were the beneficiaries of the majority of her time. When grandchildren came, she doubled down on her commitment to eternity and to legacy. From the first year of each child's life, she asked for overnight babysitting every Friday night, a commitment we as young parents were all too thankful to grant. She took her grandchildren almost every Friday night of their lives until they were seven or eight-years-old. The old lessons and Bible stories were back in action, recounted to the next generation with all her consistency and energy and the wisdom of her added experience.

When my oldest son, Sam, was five, she sat him down at the piano and began sharing her love of music. She was delighted to discover that her talent and love of music had been passed down to him. She bought us a piano so he could properly practice, and encouraged his love of music every step of the way. Sam attended church choir and sang with her as an adolescent. As a high school sophomore, he was accepted to the Governor's School for the Arts for intensive piano training. He lived in her hometown of Greenville, SC during his junior and senior year to attend the prestigious school.

As the years passed, I watched mom nurse and bury the former teenagers who had brought her into the world. They were at peace when they departed, influenced by their only daughter and having come to a belief in the God she brought home as a six-year-old child. "Sister" was the nickname her parents called my mom for almost her entire life. The name had supposedly stuck from her younger brother who never called her by her name, but it was appropriate because in many ways she had been more like a sister to them than a daughter. I wondered what thoughts went through her head as she sat next to their hospital beds, preparing to say goodbye to the kids who had grown up beside her. I wonder many more things about her today.

Where does that kind of strength originate? How does a small child with no direction or guidance grab hold of a belief and create a future for herself and her kids by sheer force of will? Does God give grace, mercy, and insight to certain people to deliver messages to the rest of us?

My mother does not answer these questions. The miracle of watching her is that she has been able to orchestrate mighty events with the plans she was given as a six-year-old child. The consistency of her life stands as one of the most singular examples I have known in this world of someone who believes what she says and acts on what she believes. It is inspiring.

Over Christmas in 2017, we rented a cabin with Mom and Dad. Both Barb and I were there, along with our spouses and all six of Mom's grandchildren. After dinner on the first night in the house, the whole family gathered around to play games and open presents. The final gift presentation was from Mom to each of her six grandchildren, ages 11 to 21. An envelope for each contained $300 and a one-page letter, which Barb read aloud as tears flowed down her face. It captures perfectly the person that I watched more than any other in my life:

Dearest Grandchildren,

Granddaddy's money from us this year as usual is for you to spend as you wish and enjoy to the fullest. But this year we want to begin a tradition for you that I know will be the source of some of the greatest joy of your lives. It will encourage your loving hearts to crave more experiences described below and I hope you will arrange your priorities in life to always be able to do these sorts of things.

I am giving you each $300 this Christmas with this stipulation: Not one penny is to be spent on yourself, but it will be the greatest gift if you do what I ask this year. Use this money to bring aid or joy to someone else throughout this year, and write down the experience every time, every detail. Then when we get together next Christmas you can share with us all that happened in 2018.

This is going to require you to be very observant of people around you, and clandestine in your skill of giving without any recognition or expectation of return. If you can, make your gifts secretly, but always personally chosen carefully according to a need you have observed. Sometimes it can take the form of just a tiny gift....a flower, a piece of candy, a cup of coffee...or a meal you pay for in a restaurant or cash you know is needed for a special thing. Sometimes the smallest thing, such as a note of appreciation to someone having a hard time is the greatest gift!

You know we will continue to give to you for your needs throughout the years for as long as we can...but I know you will have a great time doing this giving. Sharing your stories with us will bring us joy. Give your money and give yourselves to helping bring more joy to a broader world and you will NEVER lack for joy in your lives.

Much, much love,

Grandmommy

James P. "Buck Clardy"
circa 1944

Sandra with Father, Grandfather, & Great Grandfather
circa 1950

As President of Girls Nation with President John F. Kennedy
Oval Office (1962)

Sandra with Ben Breazeale

JENNIFER STEELE

By: Tracey Steele

One of the toughest pieces to write is the story of my mother because it is, in essence, the story of me. For as long as I can remember, family, friends, teachers, church members, and strangers alike have echoed that Jennifer Steele and I are spitting images; there's no denying I am her child—or if the light hits just right, the angle is spot on, and you tilt your head a little to the left—I am her younger sister ;). I never quite saw—and quite frankly, from time to time I still don't see—the physical resemblance, and in my teens and early 20s I vehemently denied having any of her personality traits.

Growing up, my parents played a mean game of "Good Cop, Bad Cop." My mother always played the heck out of that bad cop role. I'm talking repeat Academy Award winning performances, or going toe to toe with Mister in *The Color Purple*. She was that good. Okay, perhaps that's a *little* extreme, but the point is, in my younger years, I loathed comparisons to her; who wants to grow up to be exactly like her mean cop mom? Not I, or so I thought. But as time has passed, and I have matured—thank Jehovah Jireh for that— I have learned that my mother and I are far more similar than different, and these similarities go far beyond skin deep. I am truly blessed to be cut from her cloth. And perhaps that's the first lesson I've learned; good comes in all shapes, sizes, and packages. And even when we're too naïve to understand it, there are people—hey Mom and Dad—looking out for us, challenging us, and cheering for us, even though their cheers may be disguised as tough love cloaked in seriousness.

And though it seemed it at times, Mom wasn't always *that* serious. She was, however, unwaveringly persistent in her pursuit of excellence—a mastery of knowledge and a mastery of self.

For as long as I can remember and even well before I was born, my mother has been a voracious consumer of information. She'd often relate stories of her younger years; she took her studies seriously and endeavored to learn as much as possible. When in class, she'd be one of the first ones to raise her hand and offer a point of view. She read. She studied. She learned. She read some more.

And when she went off to college she practiced the same classroom and study habits. As a freshman at Dillard University, Jennifer sought out and maintained a work-study job at the campus library, which also happened to be where she met her future husband, but that's another story for another day. Jennifer was committed to learning as much as possible and placed herself in environments that supported this goal.

Fast-forward many years; this lesson became real to me, as I watched my mother learn to speak Spanish. In the summer of 1997, I prepared to enter seventh grade. Part of those preparations included selecting a language to study over the next two years. I selected Spanish—and I was pumped; it was one of the first times I could select my own classes. With a grin from ear-to-ear, I eagerly and proudly announced my selection to my mom. With just as much excitement, she informed me, "Tracey, I'll join you. I want to learn Spanish too." I was perplexed and mostly focused on how my mom was copying me.

The reality was, Delta had just begun expanding its Latin American footprint. With multiple routes coming online and others slated to come online soon, there was a pressing need for additional Spanish-speaking flight attendants. I'm not sure whether her goal was to be Spanish language certified, but she wanted to work these routes, communicate with her passengers, and understand them and their culture.

So began Jennifer's quest to learn Spanish—our quest to learn Spanish. And learn we did. Initially, my mom began to self-study. She purchased beginner Spanish instruction books and would spend evenings and weekends reading and practicing. She'd incorporate Spanish language TV and ask me to practice with her. Initially, all was well, because after all, I was a beginner too. But over time, I began to outpace her learning; I would dissect her pronunciation or comment on her limited vocabulary. I had Spanish class two or sometimes three days a week, and challenging assignments to go with it. Despite my critical approach, she still pressed on; still reading her books, watching Spanish language TV, and reciting common phrases and questions.

Looking to accelerate her learning, add more structure, and help me along the way, Jennifer found *us* a Spanish teacher, Mr. Elias. Visiting this older Hispanic man who lived on the complete opposite side of Cobb County became our routine. Every week, we'd venture to his downtown Marietta home, sit around a patio table overlooking the community pool—with a few other budding students—and receive our weekly instruction.

He had us reciting our vowels, "aah, aaay, eee, oh, ooo... pa-pa-pa-pa." Repetition is, after all, the mother of learning. We'd recite this together, separately, alternating before moving into sentences and conversation. Those books my mom bought to self-study were resurrected for class with Mr. Elias. He'd have us read sentences and ask us about what we had read. As I watched my mom practice, I observed that responding to Mr. Elias' prompts was no easy feat. As she processed her thoughts, I could see her trying to translate them into Spanish. It was disjointed. She'd get a few words out. Think. Hesitate. Then get a few more out. That's when Mr. Elias encouraged her to "see the screen." He suggested to my mom that she imagine the words that she wanted to speak scrolling across a screen. Deliberately, but keeping steady pace, he encouraged her to speak the words she saw. What started slowly became her ticket to improving her Spanish. My mom continued to see the screen and the words started to flow faster. And with continued practice, her speech improved.

And that was key. My mother failed in front of me. She failed often. Despite potential embarrassment, she was resolved to learn this language and her persistence did not go unnoticed.

Although learning was slow, it was steady. She continuously challenged herself, working almost all Latin American routes exclusively. After flying in from Caracas, she'd burst through the door gushing about how she asked someone about his or her day and in turn they asked about hers. She'd recite all questions and responses, half giggling, half snickering, both gleeful exaltations that she'd sought to understand and had been successfully understood.

I think she fed off these experiences. My mom would regularly work Latin America trips. Caracas and Lima were her go to routes, and on her trips she would continue to practice Spanish with passengers, pilots, crewmembers, and anyone she met while in these cities.

Just when she got into a groove, my Mom kicked it up a notch; realizing she needed in be in an environment conducive to learning, my mom planned a Spanish immersion trip and invited me to come along. In the summer of 1998, we flew to Antigua; a small town nestled in southern Guatemala. For one week, we balanced focused language instruction with local cultural excursions. We'd start each day with six hours of one-on-one language instruction, take a brief break, and then round out the afternoon with all sorts of activities from coffee farm tours to bike rides through the countryside. In the evenings, we'd have dinner with our host family. How could I forget to mention the home stay component of the trip? A local Antiguan family accommodated us throughout our language immersion week.

This week enhanced the language learning process tremendously. Our host family only spoke Spanish and all language instruction and activities took place in Spanish; there were no pauses for English discussions, unless of course my mom and I had a brief conversation between us. Further, the immersion week gave us both a glimpse into the culture connected to the language we were endeavoring to learn and the people facilitating this learning.

That trip netted results. I recall seeing my mom speak with more confidence and take more chances with the language. Still, continuous practice is what helps sustains results. After that initial immersion, my mom planned more. We took a mother daughter trip to Costa Rica, enjoying a week of Spanish immersion in San Jose. My mom also planned some solo immersion ventures, traveling to San Jose on her own. Little by little, her Spanish—and confidence—continued to improve.

How my mom learned Spanish became a way of life. What resonated is how she maximized all of the resources at her disposal and created countless opportunities to learn. She did not let speaking mistakes or limited language knowledge slow her down. She did not wait until the conditions were perfect; instead, she identified a goal and took immediate action toward realizing it. She created the learning environments that would best help her to grow and focused her energy on positive outcomes, feeding off compliments from strangers, one on one conversations, and other incremental successes.

While my mom never became fluent in Spanish, she grew to become highly conversational. What she did master—and showed me along the way—is how to relentlessly pursue knowledge in the face of all obstacles.

As I was busy getting the lessons around the relentless pursuit of knowledge, my mom was fast at work learning and showing me another critical lesson—how to master oneself. In my younger years—the days spent in California and the early ones in Georgia—my mom would be easily agitated and have a short fuse. Perhaps, she just had limited tolerance for my antics! :)

Regardless, around 1999—my freshman year of high school—I began to notice a change in her. As a family of faithful attendees of Turner Chapel AME Church, we started attending events and services at the local Unity Church at my mom's urging. The Unity Church encourages exploring spiritual principles by taking a positive approach to life. It emphasizes seeking to accept the good in all people and events. When we first started attending Unity events, I thought we were just visiting another church. What I did not understand at the time was how the messages of positivity and self-actualization were being received, internalized, and put into action by my mom.

Along with attending Unity services and events, my mom started to read prosperity-themed literature. Books and writings by Florence Scovel Shinn would be all over our home. Once, when I was having a rough time, my mom passed me *The Game of Life and How to Play It,* one of Shinn's novels. It focuses on giving and receiving, explaining that whatever one sends out in words and deeds will be returned to him or her. My mom kept these teachings handy. I not only saw her applying these principles, but encouraging me to practice them too.

My mom started incorporating meditation into her daily routine as well. At first, she would wake up early in the morning to practice mindfulness. Then, she advanced to twice a day, practicing every morning and evening. She would encourage me to join her, and from time to time, I would. No matter what, she was resolved to dedicating herself to mastering how to control her breath, her thoughts, and to set intentions. And through daily observation and gentle nudging, I learned how to do the same.

Jennifer Steele, in teaching herself, taught me; she showed me what the pursuit of excellence looks like in two of the most important areas of life: the pursuit of knowledge and the pursuit of self-control. As I look back, these experiences with her and lessons learned are things that I carry with me today. I approach almost everything I do with laser focus, using all of my resources to learn as much as possible to ensure the best possible outcome. I pair this approach to learning, with an overall positive outlook on all situations, knowing that there is good in all things and that I must seek the good in all that I experience and do. This way of life has carried me through, and I attribute it all to Jennifer Steele leading by example. Although, in my younger years, I denied having Jennifer Steele's looks and personality traits, I can no longer deny either. And I'm glad. I look like Jennifer; I act like Jennifer; and I would have it no other way.

Jennifer and Tracey

The Women We Watched

ROSE MARY RICHARDSON

By: Tigerron Wells

I'd rather see a sermon than hear one any day;
I'd rather one should walk with me than merely tell the way.
The eye is a better pupil, more willing than the ear;
Fine counsel is confusing, but example is always clear,
And the best of all the preachers are the men who live their creeds,

For to see a good put in action is what everybody needs.

I can soon learn how to do it if you will let me see it done;
I can watch your hand in action, but your tongue too fast may run.

And the lectures you deliver may be very wise and true,
But I'd rather get my lesson by observing what you do.
For I may misunderstand you and the high advice you give,
But there is no misunderstanding how you act and how you live.

When I see a deed of kindness, I am eager to be kind.
When a weaker brother stumbles, and a strong man stands behind
Just to see if he can help him, then the wish grows strong in me
To become as big and thoughtful as I know that friend to be.

And all travelers can witness that the best of guides today
Is not the one who tells them, but the one who shows the way.

One good man teaches many; men believe what they behold;

One deed of kindness noted is worth forty that are told.
Who stands with men of honor learns to hold his honor dear,
For right living speaks a language which to everyone is clear.
Though an able speaker charms me with his eloquence, I say,
I'd rather see a sermon than hear one any day.
– Edgar A. Guest

This fine composition, crafted by the poet Edgar A. Guest, is one of my all time favorites. And while the poem makes generous use of the masculine pronouns "his" and "him," the sermon of example that has most impacted my life is the one that was "preached" by my mother, Rose Mary. As I would come to find out, it is a sermon that she learned from the women she watched, and would go on to "preach" it masterfully to her children.

Rose Mary Dennis was the first-born child of Elizabeth Dennis, my Grandma Liz. Grandma Liz was just a teen when Mom was born, so Mom was raised by her great-grandmother, Elersha "Essie" Dennis, in Prosperity, South Carolina. Grandma Essie was a woman small in stature, but, according to Mom, stern and resolute in her manner. Living to the blessed age of 106-years-old, she was around for a good number of my younger years. I remember she would sit quietly in the big chair in her living room next to her piano as I shadow-boxed some unknown invisible foe in the mirror that hang from her wall, or as I fed logs of wood into her cast iron stove. Her independence and entrepreneurship as well as the spirituality and work ethic of other women in the family set a powerful example for Rose Mary. She would later set a similar example for her children.

When Rose was a young woman, still in high school, she met and began a relationship with my father, Ronald Wells, of Newberry, South Carolina. They loved each other deeply, and soon decided that they would marry. On November 21, 1973, they married and set out to start their lives together.

Five years after exchanging vows, Rose became pregnant with a baby boy. On Thanksgiving Day, November 23, 1978, I made my debut. At 9 lbs, 8ozs, labor was difficult, and I eventually needed to be removed by cesarean section. As I've always heard the story, the family waited with baited breath until receiving word of my birth before they ate the traditional Thanksgiving meal that day.

Prior to my birth, Alex Haley's now famous historical fiction Roots had been made into a popular television miniseries. My father was so impressed with one of the rites performed in the story, that within a year of my birth, on a clear starry night, he took me into the front yard of his childhood home at 718 Hunt Street in Newberry, SC, held me up to the stars, and proclaimed: "Behold, the only thing greater than you."

Now, I am certain that it was my mother and father's fervent desire that they would go forward together as a family, every day working to manifest this great hope of a strong family foundation into which to propel one child and perhaps other children to greatness. Unfortunately, as is sometimes the case, the forces that far too often make victims of marital unions felled my parents' marriage, and they divorced just one year after my birth.

It is said that enduring divorce is very much like experiencing the death of a loved one. I guess that makes sense in a number of different ways. Where two have endeavored to become one, and have behaved, as best they could, as one in partnership and companionship, only to be put asunder - that is an unavoidably traumatic experience. I feel some liberty speaking authoritatively on this subject, having experienced divorce myself. I can attest to the sense of loss, and the sometimes disconcerting and confusing feelings that it can bring, particularly for those who share a child or children with the former mate. For it is in those situations where despite the end of the union between the once separate wholes, ties continue to bind through the children making it difficult to fully mourn and move on from the loss as in situations where only inanimate possessions are in need of partition.

While I have not yet stumbled across it, I'm certain there is a book out there detailing or at least exploring the mental impact on the parties in those situations. Given the fact that many of us do not seek and receive the kind of guidance that should perhaps be sought following such traumatic experiences, it is likely that unaddressed trauma contributes in some way to the sometimes poor decisions made by the again-but-not-quite-fully separate halves, particularly with respect to the children.

While I feel some liberty to speak on the impact of divorce or separation, particularly where a child or children have been born into the union, I cannot begin to imagine what it was like going through this destructive experience as an African-American woman in America in 1979. And yet, my Mom soldiered on. And through the years that followed this transformative event, my mother would preach one of her greatest sermons as an example.

Forgive and Speak Life

Growing up, from time to time, Mom would say something to the effect of, "You are just like you father," or, "You are going to be like your father." And every time I heard those words or received that message, I smiled inside.

Depending on your life experiences or cultural perspective, you may be a little confused right now. Upon reading the words of the previous paragraph, your mind may have jumped to what many have come to believe to be the norm, either as a result of personal experiences, stories recounted by friends or associates, or stories magnified through popular culture media. The words, "You are just like your father," when uttered by a single mother to her male child, can only spell trouble, right? You may have even gotten a picture of a scene in your head of some exhausted and annoyed mother with a tightly furrowed brow, her left hand on her hip, and right hand balled into a tight fist with one finger pointing as she delivers the line. But that was not my reality.

You see, my mother did not wield the words of comparison to correct me. She made expert and measured use of a belt or switch for that, as infrequently as necessary, and with very few words. She never used those words of comparison to embarrass, put me down, or destroy my self-confidence. She only ever used those words to build me up. She used those words to praise me for doing something noteworthy. Scored an A on a math test? "You are smart just like your father." Got accepted into some scholarly program? "Yep, you're going to be just like your dad." So, instead of growing up feeling like there was enmity between my mother and father, and that I was somehow doomed to embody the character of a person who filled my mother with disappointment and bitterness, instead I grew up being reminded of my quality.

Now, to be fair, I must note that she wasn't spinning tales in suggesting that Dad had accomplished great things in life. A wiz at math and a strong student otherwise, he attended Kings Point Merchant Marine Academy on a full scholarship. He distinguished himself at Kings Point, and went on to have a successful career as a maritime engineer. His drive and determination no doubt came from the woman he watched, Orrie "Girlie" Wells, my Grandma Girlie. The daughter of sharecroppers, Grandma Girlie found work with a family in Newberry cleaning house and tending children, and saved her money in order to buy a house so she could move her parents off the sharecropper's land. She accomplished that goal, and then went on to raise her only child to be a high achiever.

While I thought it important to note that Mom's encouraging comparisons were not based in complete fiction, I hope this will not cause you to lose sight of the point. While Dad had achieved success and while my young mind was unable to discern the reasons that led to my parents' divorce, rest assured that there were reasons. And if Mom had allowed it, any of those reasons could have become the focus of any comments about or references to my father. But instead of succumbing to such pointless criticism, my mother chose instead to speak life.

Unlike many stories I've heard recounted from male friends raised in single-parent homes, which are far too often marked with seemingly never-ending conflict between the former loving parents, my story is, thanks in no small part to the woman I watched, markedly different.

I do not recall my mother ever uttering the word "forgiveness" when I was growing up in her care, but her actions demonstrated the peace that comes with forgiveness. It is her example that I believe has led me, in times of strife and conflict, to walk a path of forgiveness and love rather than one of vengeance.

In This Life, You Must Find Community and You Must Work

My earliest memories of childhood begin when we were living in a small house at 2309 Chappelle St. near downtown Columbia, South Carolina. In those days, when I think of my mother, most memories involve her working. She worked a lot. During the day, she would work as an administrative assistant in the Math Department at Benedict College, and in the evenings she worked as a barber, cutting hair at Toliver's Mane Event, a well-known barbershop off of North Main St. in Columbia.

During the week, when I wasn't being cared for by either Ms. Wilhelmina "Grannie" Bristow, who worked in the cafeteria at Benedict and lived in the neighboring Allen Benedict Court community, Ms. Linda Chapman who worked at Benedict Child Development Center and lived in nearby Saxon Homes, or Ms. Lillie Boatwright, who worked as a math teacher at Benedict College and lived around the corner from us in our Lincoln Park neighborhood, I spent large amounts of time in the math department computer lab at Benedict with my mother, drawing on typing paper and flying paper airplanes. When I'd get to hang out at the barbershop, I'd often sit in the back room and do my homework while Mom worked out front. I'd emerge from time to time when my stomach started grumbling and ask Mom for some money. I'd take the dollar she'd give me and walk next door to the grocery store and buy a small pack of meat I could munch on to hold me over until it was time to go.

When I wasn't either at work with Mom or being kept by one of the ladies I mentioned, I was at home with a sitter, or alone with strict orders not to so much as open the door until Mom got home. When Mom would make it home, I could tell she was tired, but I never heard her complain. If she ever cried, she only did so behind a closed door.

When I was six-years-old, Mom gave birth to my little sister, Elersha Teneka Williams, whom she named after my Grandma Essie. I was given the honor of coming up with her middle name, which I borrowed from a little girl I was soft on at the time. While my memories of that time are all positive, as an adult, I understand the additional challenges my mother likely faced as a result of our new addition. When I think of the challenges that often face two-parent households, I am rendered in awe of the determination, faith, and love it must have taken for my mother and far too many other mothers to do it on their own.

Despite her schedule, Mom often found time to engage in meaningful activities with my sister and me. Whether this took the form of a trip to Sesquicentennial Park or some activity with her Ones United group, an organization for single mothers founded by neighborhood activist and close friend Christie Savage, there was always something.

In addition to engaging in meaningful activities as a family, Mom also made sure she remained engaged with my education. Because of my November birthday, I did not reach the age of six-years-old in time to begin first grade with my natural academic cohort. Determined not to see me fall behind in any way, Mom enrolled me in the private school program at a church, Holy Spirit, which was located just outside of our neighborhood, between Colonial Drive and Lorick Park.

Despite her effort, when I later transferred from Holy Spirit into public school in second grade, I was nearly held back because of lagging reading comprehension performance. Calling again upon the community, Mom found out about a summer reading program that was being held at a nearby school. She placed me in the program that summer, and it quickly turned things around for me academically. I do not remember the names of those ladies who worked with me in that reading program, but I do remember the love and support I felt during that short period of time. With their help, I became a confident reader. As recounted by Mom, it wasn't long before the same principal who had warned that I may need to be held back was now telling her that I was going to be successful no matter where I went in life. This was the direct result of my mother's engagement as a caring adult, and the community's involvement in steering her to available resources to assist me in achieving academic success. The lessons learned from this particular example are powerful.

These sermons of work and community, and the lessons learned from watching Mom preach through her actions, have probably served me most obviously in my life. At no point in my life have I ever felt comfortable not working. Even when enrolled in college, I applied myself to my studies as if it were a job, never missing class, always striving to be on time, and always doing my work. When school was out, there was always a summer job. That was certainly because of Mom's example. The lessons regarding the importance of community have never left me, and continue to fuel my community service and charitable activity. In fact, reflection on Mom's engagement and the input and assistance from our "village" is part of what led me and my family to create Academic Angels, Inc., a charitable non-profit aimed at identifying academic resources in a community, and then helping caring, engaged adults steer the child or children they are seeking to assist towards those resources along with funds to defray the cost.

Resilience

One of the most profound sermons of example preached by my mother, and the last one I will share, is the sermon regarding resilience. You might have already detected hints of this sermon through the experiences recounted previously. However, if you haven't picked up on this critical message by now, I hope this final sermon of example will drive home the point.

When life takes away something or someone precious, do not use it as an excuse to retreat into yourself, but instead shake yourself off through service, greater service to others, and the application of your talents to the improvement of others' lives.

Thursday, April 16, 2009 started out like any other day. I walked into my office completely unaware of how substantially my world was about to change in a matter of moments. No sooner had I crossed the threshold of my office when the phone began to ring. I was still standing when I picked up the phone and answered. I was greeted by the voice of a woman on the other end of the line, indicating desperately that she needed to find my mom. There was a man at the office looking for her. He was waiting to tell her that her daughter had been involved in an automobile accident the previous night, and had not survived.

I paraphrase the caller's words, because I am sure I do not remember them verbatim, but the words I use here capture precisely how unceremoniously and bluntly I received the news that my little sister was gone. I was staggered for a moment, and rendered dazed as the reality of the message sunk in. And then my mind shifted to my mother. How was she going to take the news that the only daughter she had carried in her womb, whom she had loved and hoped for over the past 25 years, had passed from this world? I knew only one thing for sure: I was not going to let her receive that news from the mouth of a stranger.

I walked next door into my friend, mentor, and supervising partner, Dalhi Myers' office, told her what had happened and then set out to find Mom and get her to a place where we could deliver the earthshattering news. My wife and I were able to find Mom and get her to our home. My stepdad and I arrived shortly after she had gotten there. We walked into the house, and as I passed from the foyer to the kitchen, my eyes met with my Mom's from across the room. I could not conceal the awful news, and Mom seemed to read the entire story from that brief, sorrowful glance. She began to cry a mother's cry of loss - a deep and painful moan that signifies all that disappears or becomes fractured when a child is lost.

The hours and days that followed were tough to say the least. The phone calls to family members and friends forced us to experience the heartbreak over and over again. But before long, Mom's strength resumed, and she again displayed her resilience and strength under these circumstances.

I remember traveling to the funeral home after my sister's body had arrived. We were taken down a long hallway until we came to the room where Elersha's body was being held. Mom asked to go in alone to see her child's body before it was prepared for burial. She stayed in the room for some time, sitting and surveying the broken vessel that Elersha's spirit had animated just days before. When she emerged from the room, she wore a look on her face not of sorrow, but of calm acceptance. I prepared to enter the room, and she gently grabbed my hand and dissuaded me from entering, graciously preserving for me the memories of my kid sister alive and well.

Three days after we had first received the news of Elersha's passing, her life was celebrated by an overflow capacity crowd of family and friends, and her body was laid to rest near her beloved grandmother, Emma Williams, near Savannah Grove Church in Effingham, South Carolina. In the months that followed, things seemed fine for a time, and then they took a turn for the worst. Mom started to really struggle with Elersha's passing, and needed help coping. She received the help she needed, and things again appeared to be on the uncertain road back to some semblance of normal.

Mom had long worked as an executive assistant to the Superintendent of Education for the Department of Juvenile Justice, the correctional facility that houses and is responsible for educating South Carolina's wayward youth. Before long, following Elersha's passing, I became aware that Mom had begun volunteering as a mentor to young people at DJJ. Unbeknownst to me, she had also started working as a caregiver with Home Instead Senior Care. I became aware of her service with Home Instead when I was contacted by the senior care agency regarding a surprise award that they wanted to bestow upon her as caregiver of the year.

I was honored to sit at the table with the lady of the hour when she was recognized. Prior to receiving the award, stories were shared of the ways she had gone above and beyond what was expected or reasonably anticipated to serve the people she cared for. While these were stories I was hearing for the first time, they all sounded familiar. In so many ways, they were merely a continuation of what I witnessed my mother do for most of my life – help others. It was so very rewarding to be able to enjoy that evening with her. I believe it was on that evening that I knew with certainty, for the first time, that Mom would be all right. While myself and others wondered how she was holding it together, Mom had gone on and found ways to not only survive, but to thrive by helping others.

Mom mourned Elersha: my sister, her daughter, and was deeply affected by losing her so early and unexpectedly. But while the pain of her loss, and the agony of opportunity cut short were still fresh, she looked beyond herself and pulled herself out of the abyss by serving others. What an awesome lesson. What a magnificent woman.

In conclusion, I've learned valuable lessons about forgiveness, love, resilience, selflessness, compassion, and life from my mother. These were not lessons she ever sat me down and sought to impart through careful discussion, but rather they were lessons she drilled into my head and planted in my heart daily with her own personal example. What a profound impact her example has had on my life. And what an honor it is to be able to share her sermon with you.

Rose Mary Richardson

Caregiver of the Year Award
Rose Mary Richardson
2013

CATHERINE CHRISTINE STANKOVICH

By: Nicholeen Brame (Nikki)

As I recount years gone by, I call upon my memories to bring them to life in the words that follow. I wish this to be my way of honoring the Woman I Watched, my mother!

My mother, Catherine Christine Stankovich was a woman of great stature and as I fulfill each era of my life's journey, she will always remain my role model. Her heart was gentle, caring, and kind each minute of every day.

Many women shared in the desire to be like her! When she entered the room, all heads turned; she stood beautiful and confident in every setting. Aware of my mother's kindness, friends and acquaintances would reach out to her for help and support as a wife or mother going through troubled times, as she was a great listener, always with an open heart! Her love and caring for those in need and her desire to somehow make a difference in the lives of less fortunate children and the elderly was easily recognized. Her friends knew she would listen and never share the tales they told.

Many years were spent caring for her own mother and my father's mother through their painful battles at the end of their lives. Mother never complained and acted as a special care nurse with love and nurturing for both mothers until their deaths. As a child, I witnessed the love she showed daily to make them comfortable and shared stories to lighten their hearts from the pain they were feeling. Likewise, later she did the same for my grandfather who was left behind in death by my father's mother. He gave her a rough time in his last days, but she continued to care for him and overlooked his angry attitude, and before he passed, he shared his love for her. Tears in her eyes, she told him she loved him like a father and gave peace to his soul in passing. You see, he was never angry with her; he was angry that his wife passed on before him and left him behind. He loved my grandmother so much, his choice would have been his passing on first, and hers to follow years later. This was a lesson for me in unconditional love, going beyond the perspective of the here and now in my own life and identifying how I too can make a difference in the lives of others.

While she clothed me with gorgeous clothes and took me on many shopping trips to check out the latest styles, she reminded me of the importance of understanding the value of the dollar and the sacrifice that came with earning it. She chose to serve the needy; they came first for her every day. My mother's tender and caring nature wasn't simply bound by family; it was in her soul to care for everyone. She walked with a giving heart. Simple things like recycling our toys and games with children in our community. Our clothes were recycled to families in need, offered crisp and clean as quickly as we were newly clothed. She never spoke of her good deeds, however we as a family witnessed how careful she was to say things like, "The kids have grown out of these, you know they grow so fast," in an effort to keep others from feeling like it was a hand out, but simply sharing. She was very protective of her kindness as she never wanted credit or to be honored in any way. Even as a young girl it made me proud to see these children overwhelmed with joy.

As a little girl she protected me from harm, she dried my tears, she was the reason for my smiles, and gave me the opportunity to grow not only by inches, but in heart, mind, and spirit. She was a proud mother and our family was her mission in life.

Mother was always ready to cuddle and hug and sing songs and dance with me. She loved to read books, and always wanted me to be in the know, so she planned travel to new places, fun in the sun on beaches, holiday parades, movies, shopping, and special dinners out to make my childhood one to remember and enjoy. She loved riding the bus: today there is no comparison. Those on the bus were friendly and caring, many had children with them, so it was usually a fun ride where many times we would try to come up with games to play in our seats while the grown ups were sharing stories. That experience continued with Mother taking my children on bus rides. Today they speak of the fun they had with Mother and how special those times were for them; going into the city to see a movie, some shopping, and always having lunch at Murphy's in Harrisburg. It was never about what they could get, or what she would buy for them, it was just spending time with her, staying overnight with her, and having slumber parties, watching scary movies, baking cookies, going for walks, shopping at the mall, and enjoying time together with her.

As I passed through several stages of my life, each day I was reminded of the troubles in the world and how life would unfold differently than we dreamed or felt it would. Today, as I grow older, the world still appears cruel and invasive, but I always know I can somehow connect with my Mother and regain the confidence to push through the tunnel of darkness, knowing she would be by my side to see me through. I truly felt equipped with enough knowledge and the skillset that prepared me to make the best decisions possible but I would never fret if the decision I made turned out to be wrong. It was an opportunity for me to make a better decision in the future. You see, my mother taught me that growth comes with failure and bad decisions allow for making better decisions, as life is a journey of change!

While in high school at Bishop McDevitt in the city of Harrisburg, Pennsylvania, racism was rampant. My mother frowned heavily on racism and would not tolerate any such behavior within our family or friends passing through our home. There were neighbors who were good friends but who, at times crossed the line and she would stand tall and let them know our family believes in brotherly love. I can remember as a young girl my parents sitting on the front porch listening to music and chatting about their day with some of these folks whom they considered to be friends; they were always included in our family holidays. She was firm that people of different races were our brothers and sisters and should be loved and cared for as we love and care for each other! It was concerning to me that during this stage in my life I learned that injustice may be prevalent in society but even as a woman you have a voice.

She outlined for me that it was important to separate myself from the struggles and challenges she and many women before her faced to make a better way for us and to learn from them! It was apparent to me that her life was spent making a difference every day. Some stories she shared were of amazing accomplishments of women who fought for women's rights and worked tirelessly to prepare for better and less bumpy traveling roads. She wanted to infuse in me the responsibility to continue forging and opening more pathways for the young women who would follow. I was inspired daily with the knowledge that I was in control of all situations I crossed through as a woman and needed to walk with my head held high and with confidence and only look back to remember the lesson learned. As I faced each day, I knew if I chose to walk alone as opposed to following the crowd, I was strong enough to make that choice! She prepared me to handle quick detours when needed and to walk away when necessary. The gentleness of my mother's guidance and the example she lived are the reason that today I am prepared to face what life throws my way.

Her life was not always an easy one. During World War II, while my father was a Sergeant in the US Army, she soloed through years alone. She would send care packages to him and his platoon often and write daily without fail. During his time in the service, there was a long duration where she had no communication with him. On the day she received word that our father had been injured during active duty by an explosive in the field, her worst fears came to life and her faith was challenged. Once notified, weeks followed where she still had no idea how badly he was injured. Finally, she learned he had been admitted to a hospital in France. Months followed as she prayed for his release from the hospital. My memory often reminds me as did she, that in times of doubt, fear or confusion, "Life will throw you a curve ball along what appears to be a weary road, but our Lord will lift you above the hurt and reset the stage you are centered in!" Daily, she prayed her rosary for peace of heart and a solemn place for those to find when at their lowest moment. My father earned a Purple Heart and was sent home to finalize his recuperation where Mother took care of him and nursed him back to health. My mother walked this earth with great faith; a rosary in her pocket and her little hand prayer book condensed with prayers to patron saints and angels; prayers to our Blessed Mother for guidance to be a good mother, prayers to the Father, the Son, and the Holy Ghost always asking them to be in charge in her life. She spoke wisely that peace of heart only comes within a peaceful soul.

In their early years, my parents lived in a humble house on the west side of Steelton until a flood took their home, their livestock, and all their belongings. They rose to the occasion with strength and perseverance and acquired quite a bit of land in a small village called Bressler where they settled and moved the rest of their extended families. It was there that my dad built a beautiful cottage home, the first home I knew! We spent years of happiness in that home. Our grandparents were minutes away on both sides of the hills; one referred to as Grandma up the hill, my father's mother, and Grandma over the hill, my mother's mother. I mention them both because they were amazing women of faith, witness of love and life, and willingness to do whatever it took to protect their families and honor their children and grandchildren.

During my father's deployment, my mother was left alone to raise my brother. Like a well-oiled machine, she kept the family going while she worked at the Swift factory in Harrisburg, Pennsylvania preparing meats to be sold, as well as working for a time at Bethlehem Steel alongside my grandmothers where she made bullets for the war. Once my father returned home, my sister was conceived, and the family plateaued for a few years until I came along as the baby of the family. I was welcomed with open arms and spoiled beyond belief.

Before a television was introduced, we would gather in the evenings as a family around a cabinet radio listening to stories and to my parents who told us about their lives as children. It sounded amazing but so different from my childhood experiences. Very often with coffee on the stove, my mother would share stories of Croatia and read the *Zajednicar* and translate it into English. It was a Croatian Fraternal Union Newspaper started in 1904. It was fun getting the updates on what was happening in Zagreb, the town where our mother was born. She had a way of bringing it to life so much that it became a dream of mine to travel to Croatia and then take a train to Serbia, so I can visit my Croatian and Serbian roots and see if I can trace back to any locals. We followed Serbian and Croatian traditions that kept me grounded, and that still exist within our family traditions. Blessed was I to have enjoyed a life surrounded by music and dancing, encircling my heart every day. Music from records on the Victrola rang through our house each day. I have fond memories and remember giggling as my dad twirled my mom around and ending the dance with a kiss. It made me feel like the world was a great place because of so much love.

My mother was proud of her home, every inch, both inside and out. Our home was always spotless and ready for company. I remember there were always flowers in the house in several rooms and plants galore. She would say, "We need oxygen in here, be sure to water the plants kids and don't allow any dead flowers in the house. We want fresh and beautiful flowers surrounding us as a reminder of all the goodness in our lives."

She taught us that everything had a place and our job was to help everything find its place. The doors of our home were always open to anyone in need. Together she worked with my father to show us how to appreciate the land, livestock, and everyone who crossed our paths. Mom was exceptionally poetic in how she exemplified love with our dad, love of her children, love of extended parents and family, and love of neighbors and strangers near and miles away.

The holidays were filled with traditions of Croatian and Serbian history, our heritage. Mounds of food, friends, family, and neighbors who were not as blessed all gathered at our home throughout the holidays, laughing and singing joyous carols of delight. These are memories deeply embedded in my heart.

Each Sunday, we attended church at St. Mary's in Steelton and St. Nicholas Byzantine Church so we would come to understand, know, and cherish both heritages and be proud of them. Because of learning early on the differences between our church and the Serbian Church, I am open to other faiths and learning more about them. Being respectful of these heritages has allowed me to live a similar, yet very different life. However, in our families, we continue traditions throughout the year that I witnessed as I was growing up, such as the poor man's meal for Christmas Eve. Instead of a feast, our family has a sparse meal and blesses our homes welcoming Christmas into our hearts and home as a gesture to honor the birth of Jesus in the stable.

As I faced motherhood, moments of my childhood began to flow back. I was always cold and shivering waiting for the bus, watching the parade, standing outside in the winter months talking to the neighbors, playing in the snow. My Mother would wrap her coat around me while I stood in front of her. I remember the warmth of her body. Her face was soft and beautiful, the smell of her cologne and the kisses she left behind on my cheek with her rose-colored Peggy New-ton Lipstick. I knew I had her strength and confidence to lean on as I faced stormy waters of uncertainty. Although I didn't know what true strength was until I gave birth of my first-born daughter, Christy Anne. As the miracle unfolded before my eyes, I finally understood the meaning and truth of life.

During my pregnancy with my first born, it proved to be a special time for me as my father had been very ill with cancer for several years. He was told he would not live to see his granddaughter born. He stood strong and said no one tells him what he knows in his heart is possible. Watching my parents with the baby while feeding her and giving her evening baths through the late hours of the night with such tenderness and care was the moment that the tight bond I witnessed as a child with their love for me came full circle as an adult. My mother's strength followed again with my pregnancy and the birth of my second child, Scott Christopher. Once again, I witnessed her strength as she pulled through and sought to aspire to remain strong and an example of strength as my father passed away.

My mother was in a full leg brace due to a broken tibia in her leg from a fall; however, she was right there and present to nurture along-side of my new son and me. She would smile and remind me that each miracle lightens the pain surrounding it, so not to worry. Despite her excruciating pain and the struggle to walk across the room, she took her time and lightened the pain.

As the children aged and we traveled through several states of residence including Kansas and Colorado and visits back and forth, my mother remained by my side. We traveled to be with her almost weekly and she, in turn, traveled to be with me and my children for long periods of time. The best years of my life were watching her love on my babies and witnessing her being first in the hearts of my chil-dren. She would play games with them or sneak in a scary movie. She loved them and she would engage with them in anything they wanted to do. She welcomed their questions and interest in the olden days and stories about my father and their lives. The smiles on the children's faces when they were with her and the smile she proudly wore when by their sides always brought back memories of my childhood days with her and how I so loved being loved by her passion, wondrous heart, and genuine spirit.

One sunny afternoon as my mother and I sat together, outside enjoying the summer breeze, I reminded her of my childhood dream to have three children when I grew up. I then told her that I was thinking of having my third child. She looked lovingly at me because I was 39 years old and during that period 39 was not considered a prime birthing age. Then after a brief period of silence she said, "God will bring his touch forward and I will pray you through your wonderful dream."

My parents often had preconceived notions of who their grandchildren would become and while my father received his cheerleader in Christy Anne, he hoped for one to be similar to him in loving animals, gardening, and woodworking. My mother reminded me during this trying time that he also hoped he'd have a grandson who would be his little football player. Mother didn't have the same kind of fiery requests for her grandchildren, as long as they walked in faith she would be proud.

After hearing her words, I stood firm at my crossroad and decided to have another child. Maybe my father would get his football player to fulfill all his grandchildren dreams or maybe hers would be a priest in the family. With confidence, she shared these memories of hope. Her words of faith rang through and God showed the way! My youngest son, John Anthony was conceived on the night of my mother's death. In the saddest moment of my life, God's hand touched me because of my mother's true belief and faith. Delivered to me was my third miracle, one to enjoy and guide through life and who together with my other children, would bring me years of love, gentle moments, and more knowledge and love!

Mother spoke many times of the blessings of her grandchildren and wanted me to know that if she was not given the chance to love on my third miracle, that she would meet him and protect him until he was in my arms. I hold onto that belief, because my entire life was written and guided by this amazing Woman that I Watched.

What I never knew was possible was the promise that I would be blessed with two beautiful miracle grandchildren, Edith Simone and Brooklyn Carter. Mother used to say, your dreams will come full circle when you welcome your grandchildren into the world and into your arms as they are your strength and witness to a fulfilled life in Christ. When I looked into the eyes of my grandchildren, and my children I easily burst into tears. Tears of joy, tears of the unknown, tears of years passing me by, and I see them gazing back, as if to say, "Nana, it will be OK."

Mother always said that through your children's babies, you will enjoy and re-live your young life once again in your old age and witnessing the children you brought into this world living, loving, and nurturing their children and their sibling's children is a powerful reality that not all will experience. Be Blessed!

I recognize that the miracle of life has unfolded for me and there is nothing more beautiful than a family that believes, prays, and stays together through all the times, happy and sad, crossing troubled waters hand in hand. I pray their hands stay connected as their hearts reach new heights and they never forget their beginnings and see each other to the end!

Mother was a strong believer in those that walked in faith before us being the ones who have paved the roads for our travels through life, so it has always been important to me to be an example of love, prayer, repentance when needed, and caring for others, so my children and grandchildren would enjoy the happiest of times in their lives. I feel safe in knowing that my mother continues to walk daily with me, her angel wings folded gently over me in times of need, crisis, and tears!

I sit in confidence knowing that it was her example of caring, nurturing, and boundless love that was in every twinkle of her eye; that paved my journey. These are small, cherished treasures portrayed through my lifetime as evidence of all the times I felt my heart beating outside my body when I peered into their loving eyes. Today when I close my eyes, I can still see her smiling at me and know she is just a memory away.

In wonderment, I lament my thanks to my mother who prepared me for life, it's trials and tribulations, it's blessings, and it's curveballs, but more so how to be a mother of genuine love, heart, understanding, and forgiveness. I cherish my children, my miracle grandchildren who without God's intervention and touch would not be in my life!

As I grow in mind, age, and body, and burst in heart, I look back over my mother's life, one that I hold close! In my moments as I walk on earth, memories pull me back often to realize all the minutes, days, and years I was present, just to appear today as not enough time spent building dreams with my parents.

It rings true in my daily life as I look inward and onward with a tearful glistening eye of my children, grandchildren, and their family lives.

Can it be that I already feel cheated out of time with them and know that some day they too will face the memory of just 'not enough time? In wonderment, were the shallow tears in my mother's eyes due to just not enough time?

Catherine Christine Stanokovich
(1914-1989)

OLLIE HALL BECKETT JOHNSON

By: Evette Beckett-Tuggle

I watched her wash the dishes in our little kitchen. It was the summer of 1964. I wasn't quite eight-years-old. We were living in a small house in the working class section of Locust Valley, a small, unincorporated, largely affluent hamlet on the North Shore of Long Island. She had her back to me, so I couldn't see her face when I made my declaration. She stood at the kitchen sink humming a gospel song. Mom sung often, being a member of the First Baptist Church choir. On Saturdays especially, she would have the gospel radio station on WLIB while she did her housework. The music coming out of the radio featured great gospel choirs and soloists like Andraé Crouch and the Edward Hawkins Singers. They would sing songs like *Through It All* and *Oh Happy Day*. The volume of the radio was always turned up very loud so that she could hear it as she moved about the house, cleaning from room to room. Directly in front of her above the kitchen sink was a window that looked out onto the patio and backyard. The sunlight shone brightly through the window and cast a glow around her head.

"I want to be saved," I said in a very small voice. My mother turned away from the window and looked down at me.

"What did you say? You want to be what? Do you even know what that means...to be saved?" she asked in rapid-fire succession. Then she proceeded to tell me what it meant to be saved, how serious it all was, and how serious I would have to be about Jesus, baptism, and salvation.

I stood confident in my little seven-year-old body and told her, once again, after her lecture was over, that I wanted to be saved. And so one night later that summer, I was the youngest of those clad in white gowns and white towel turbans at the baptismal pool of the Union Baptist Church in Hempstead, New York. I watched my mother's face, a face growing confident in whom I was and who I was becoming, as she wept.

My mother strongly influenced my faith in God being a woman of faith herself. My parents were Christians and attended church regularly. Mom bought me books about God and taught me to pray. As a little girl growing up in the 1950s and 1960s, I was instructed to sit in the front pew of our church in my Sunday best organza dresses puffed up with crinoline slips; anklet lace socks and patent leather shoes adorned my feet and were paired with a matching "pocketbook." My mother loved to get dressed up and to dress me. With my knees generously greased and hands neatly folded on my lap in obedient attention, I sat quietly, as instructed, so that she could watch me. I was happy to do so, because what she didn't know was I was watching her too. My mother had a strong, alto voice and as I looked up into the choir loft, I could pick it out among the dozen or so voices singing the anthem, "*Let Mt. Zion Rejoice*" with perfectly O-shaped mouths.

I watched her get filled with the Holy Spirit and "get happy" in church which meant she might sometimes throw her head back and shout and cry. Once, while sitting at the piano in church, one of Mom's many magnificent church hats flew out of the choir loft as she got happy and threw her head back. My father ran to be by her side and to retrieve her hat. I was more concerned that she might fall backward with her hat and so I was not at all amused, as other children were, by what I saw. Quite frankly, this "getting happy" stuff scared me half to death. I really didn't see what was so happy about people screaming and crying out loud. It looked like they were sad or in pain or something. It was bad enough to see other women in the church do this, but I didn't like seeing my Mom this way. Years later, one of my brothers admitted he stopped going to church because it scared him too. It would always startle me and send a jolt from my spine up to the back of my head. At seven, I knew I wanted to be saved, but I hadn't matured enough in my faith or reconciled in my mind the "getting happy" part. So I started watching her to see if I could detect some sign of when it might happen again so I could prepare myself for another jolt.

In addition to singing in the choir, Mom was a leader in the church, often taking the role of chair of a committee or event. She led committees like the Senior Choir, Pastor's Aid, Willing Workers, and the Church Anniversary. In her later years, she was given the title of "Mother of the Church." She also played the piano and in her sixties, became a church musician. Mom was given a special gift – a God-given gift, really, of playing the piano by ear. None of us really knew just how special this gift truly was until decades later when she was in her eighties.

Her gift was remarkable. Mom could play anything she heard once. She could hear any genre of music on the radio - gospel, pop, classical - then sit down at the piano and play it. It did not always flow easily at first, but she would always work it out until it did, adding harmonizing chords to round it out. One of my favorite songs that Mom would play this way was the Gershwin song "Summertime." She would play it with harmonizing chords and sing along. I used to watch her long, graceful fingers gliding across the ivory keys. I used to think, *Wow! How does she do that?*

It is because of her remarkable gift and deep love of music that I am also musical. Mom was so musical, she didn't need an instrument. She used to demonstrate how to do "Hambone" which she learned as a child by slapping the front and back of her right hand against her right thigh in rapid, rhythmic movements. I quickly learned that "Hambone" was both a verb and a noun, as the movements were accompanied by the lyrics to "Hambone."

Hambone, Hambone, have you heard?
Papa's gonna buy me a mockingbird
And if that mockingbird don't sing
Papa's gonna buy me a diamond ring
And if that diamond ring don't shine
Papa's gonna take it to the five and dime
Hambone. Hambone...

My mother's interest in music was quite diverse. She introduced me to Beethoven after hearing one of his compositions on a classical radio station and working it out on the piano. She insisted that I learn how to play "the right way" and paid for me to have piano lessons from one of our church musicians. Beethoven's "Fur Elise" was the first classical piano piece I learned to play. Years later, when I was about ten-years-old, my mother took me to a concert at our local high school. The concert pianist, André Watts was performing. I was very impressed by the fact that he was a black man. I hadn't been exposed to too many people of color who played classical music at that time. So seeing him made me feel very proud. After the show, my mother took me backstage and we met Mr. Watts. We shook his hand. That was a special moment that we shared and a real highlight for us both.

I did a lot of watching growing up being the youngest person in my family. I grew up around relatives that were mostly older than me. My father was nearly seventeen years older than my mother. He was 47 and my mother was just shy of 31 when I was born. My four siblings were seven to eleven years older than me. I was taught to be quiet and respectful of my elders and so I did a lot of listening and observing. I took note.

My mother was always fascinating for me to watch because she was a beautiful woman to look at. She had honey golden skin and beautiful long hair. Her hands were delicate and graceful and she had a sexy laugh. My father and siblings all adored her and women envied her. In short, my mother rocked. Mom was humble about it, though, which added to her appeal. She was a shy introvert and didn't grow up with the sense of self-confidence that I had as a child.

My mother, Ollie Leon Hall, was born in Burlington, North Carolina in 1925, the seventh of eight children. When she was a little girl, she used to bump into things a lot. It took her family a while to figure out that she needed glasses. She also stuttered as a child, but as she grew older, she grew out of it. She was a tall, skinny child with very long legs. She used to play basketball and loved to climb trees. One of her aunts gave her the nickname "Jim" and it stuck. All of her friends and family called her by her nickname. Many decades later, "Jim" was softened to "Gem" by my mother's second husband, who mistakenly thought everyone was saying Gem instead of Jim. I thought this new nickname better fit the essence of her adult personality. God gave my mother a special gift of playing the piano by ear, and it was a source of comfort, pride, and confidence for her to use and demonstrate this talent to others as she grew out of her awkward adolescence into womanhood. She left the south, like so many of her contemporaries, in the 1940s during the Great Migration, in search of a better life. She moved north to Long Island, New York. At age 18 she married my father. Together, they raised five children and worked as blue-collar laborers - my father as a construction worker and my mother doing "day work" as a maid for several prominent families on Long Island.

While other children went to camp, I used to accompany my mother to her various jobs during my summers off from school. She used to clean houses for three different families each week. I was not the athletic, outdoors type, so I didn't mind. I preferred being with her in these settings to summer camp. The homes were mansions with beautifully manicured lawns and tasteful decor. I used to watch her on her hands and knees scrubbing someone else's bathtub.

She would hum while she worked. Years later, whenever I was faced with an obstacle to overcome in college or in my professional life, all I had to do was think of the image of my mother on her hands and knees toiling so that she could clothe, house, and feed me and my four siblings, and I would snap out of my pity party. It humbled me to think of her laboring this way for us. I could see her pretty face and straight cut bangs sometimes falling into her face. I would watch her move deftly through the rooms in these houses, taking care not to get in the way of the inhabitants. She would sequester me to some quiet place in the house to draw or to read the stories in my *Weekly Reader*, an educational magazine for children that she subscribed to during the summer. Sometimes, with permission from her employers, I would practice my piano pieces on their grand piano. Mom made sure I had piano lessons so that I would learn to read music, although many times I tried to play by ear like she did. I thought that was a cool thing to do. In most of these homes, she was about the same age as the women of the house and they would confide all sorts of personal details of their lives in my mother. They were comfortable with my mother and with having me tag along with her during the summer. So occasionally, they would invite me to go swimming or horseback riding with their children, neither of which I wanted to do. I preferred to stay indoors with Mom.

Mom was a confidante to all sorts of women. Black, white, rich, poor, young, or elderly, they approached her from all stations of life. I think they liked gazing into her beautiful face and hearing her distinctive laugh. Mom was an attentive listener and gave good counsel. She likened herself to a sort of shrink. She would wait patiently before providing her commentary, reprimand, or advice to whatever it was they were saying. Sometimes, I would see her lean over and speak in hushed tones so I wouldn't overhear what she was saying. Then all of a sudden, she would let out this uncharacteristically loud, triumphant laugh. Really, I was jealous I wasn't in on the conversation.

I guess Mom was the confidante for all five of her children. She certainly was my confidante. As a teenager and adult, I told her about every skeleton there was in my closet. It was a bit risky telling her some of the things I did, but I trusted her. I knew that while she may not agree with my course of action, decision, or judgment, she would still love me unconditionally. She told me so. I felt safe in her confidence that somehow everything would be all right after I divulged all of my drama to her. My mother was my best friend. She could read me like a book. She knew instinctively when something was wrong just by looking at me, and she would call me out on it.

I believe that mothers know their children so well they can speak them into their "becoming." One day when I was about twenty, she said to me, "You're a writer." It was as if she was making some profound declaration. It was like she was calling me out and prophesying my destiny. I said to her, "Mom the best writers write from their experiences. I'm too young to write. I haven't experienced much in my young life. When I'm in my fifties, then I would have experienced something worth writing about." Flash forward thirty-four years: one day my daughter and I were cleaning out my mother's house preparing it for sale. I was clearing out a pile of shoes and clothing that had fallen onto the floor of her bedroom closet. At the bottom of the pile, I pulled out an old cigar box, blew off the dust that had collected on the top, and lifted the lid. Inside were a stack of letters I wrote to my mother when I was twenty and living as a student abroad, in my junior year of college, in London. I had no idea that she did this. My prophetic mother saved my letters, I believe, as fuel for my writing! She gave me a gift of memories to reflect on in my fifties. She gave me my "experiences" to write about.

In African-American churches across America, many congregants who worked in humble, blue-collar jobs during the week held positions of high esteem in the church on Sunday. They were the preachers and Sunday school teachers, the deacons, the trustees, and the choir directors. This was especially true of my childhood experience growing up in the First Baptist Church of Glen Cove, New York. My mother was one of those leaders. She commanded respect in her church, in her community, and in the way she carried herself. Like so many women during that time, she would arrive at church dressed to the nines! Back then, many of the fine clothes she wore were hand-me-downs from the white women that employed her. She paired these garments with magnificent, ornate hats that she purchased along with gloves, shoes, matching handbags, and beautiful costume jewelry. Mom was sharp and she knew it. She always took pride in her appearance and raised my sister and me to do the same. I remember once as a teenager she scolded me for wearing too much black (which I still do today not in a Gothic way but in a Chanel or Audrey Hepburn chic way) and she also scolded me for not wearing enough makeup! Imagine being the teenager who had the mother that encouraged you to "put the lipstick on." That was my mother.

When Mom was at home, she was often in the kitchen cooking. She had seven mouths to feed with a doting husband and five growing children. In the morning before we would go to school, she would rise early to make us a hot breakfast that consisted of Cream of Wheat, Maypo, or Wheaties, "the breakfast of champions," with hot milk and bananas! Among her best-loved dinner entrees were her lasagna, chicken and dumplings, and corn pudding. The best of Mom's homemade desserts were her blueberry cobbler, banana pudding with vanilla wafers, and homemade vanilla ice cream that she would crank with vanilla, eggs, cream, salt, and ice in a wooden bucket on the Fourth of July. I used to assist my mother when she entertained at home and watched her pull out her beautiful green and gold Chinoiserie secretary desk that she used as a server, her finest. I'd watch her organize her chafing dishes and serving utensils on the dining room table. She would put handwritten slips of paper in place of each dish, bowl, and platter so she would know exactly where to place each food item when she was ready to serve. When it was time to clean up, she would use tea towels to place the freshly cleaned China, silverware, and crystal to dry. I always thought these items looked elegant drying on white tea towels. This process of organizing with notes and cleaning up with tea towels is one I've incorporated into my own party preparation and still do today.

Looking back, I was influenced by my mother in so many ways. Not only did her abiding faith, love of entertaining and music leave a strong imprint on me, but her sense of humor is one that I recognize in some of the things that I do and say. During the 1970s when streaking became popular, my mother decided to participate in this act of freedom, privately, just for fun. One day while my sister and I were watching television in the basement of our house, Mom came running down the stairs with just her socks and a scarf flowing from her beautiful neck, passing us without so much as a glance, into the laundry room and back up the stairs again. My sister and I looked at each other in disbelief and cracked up laughing. Mom was hilarious! Mom was an absolute lady, but she could do and say some things that would make you clutch your pearls. That spice is one of the many things about her that I love so much.

Ever since I could remember, my mother took care of things. She took care of the house and her family - all of us, including our father. My father could not read or write. He grew up in Virginia, the son of a sharecropper who died when my father was nine-years-old. My father dropped out of school to help his family tend the land and never went back to finish his education. Later, when he married my mother, Mom handled all of the financial and business transactions in the family. She wrote the checks and handled all correspondence. When my father was diagnosed with colorectal cancer, Mom took care of him, nursing him until he died at the age of 79. She took care of her oldest sister when she was diagnosed with Alzheimer's and eventually brought my aunt into her home to live for more than 10 years before she died. Mom was a caregiver and a nurturer.

Five years after my father died, Mom remarried at the age of 68. My sister and I watched her walk regally down the aisle of the church while we stood as her matrons of honor with our three brothers, each of them waiting patiently to take their turn in accompanying her to the alter. She was a glowing majesty clothed in green and ivory silk brocade. Mom had violins playing and hundreds of people in attendance at her wedding. I watched her jump the broom and she looked so happy. Although I loved my father dearly and was pegged as a "Daddy's Girl," I was thrilled for my mother to have found yet another good man to spend the rest of her life with. I was proud that this once shy woman went all out in her sixties and had a big wedding with all the bells and whistles. I thought, "Wow! What an inspiration!"

It used to bother me that Mom worked as a maid, particularly in my teen years. I thought she had the intellect to do far greater things and couldn't understand why she didn't feel the same. It was during that time that I was accepted into a private, Quaker school on full scholarship surrounded by wealthy white kids from prominent families like the ones my mother cleaned for. I remember feeling awkward when I went to their homes, greeted by their black maids and asked by their parents at the dinner table what my parents did for a living. When I confronted my mother about this, she sat me down one day and rehearsed with me just what I should say. She said, "Tell them I work as a private secretary." I remember trying this explanation a few times and not feeling so good about it or about myself afterward. How could I be ashamed of my own mother and what she did for a living? She was good, decent, hard working, God-fearing, and along with my father, provided well for her five children. Mom finished high school and married Dad at eighteen and started having babies at nineteen. She never went to college. Instead, she took one of the few jobs offered to colored women during the 1940s. I was afraid because of her relatively low status job in comparison with the parents of my white and black schoolmates that they might look down on her and on me and I would not be able to tolerate it. I remember thinking; "I should be ashamed of myself for even feeling this way and approaching my mother with these silly insecurities!" In truth, I was ashamed of hurting my mother's feelings, even though she played it off and never admitted that I did.

As I grew into womanhood and into my own person and learned about all my mother and father had gone through in the struggle for civil rights and human dignity, none of which they ever talked to me or my siblings about, I realized that the industrious work ethic, quiet strength, and balanced perspective that others saw in me came from the experiences I had through my parents, in particular, my mother. Instead of wanting to conceal what she did, I found myself looking forward to telling others so they could see just how rich and textured my family really was. I am the product of a success story. My father and mother were conquerors during the Great Migration, had persevered, and were victorious. They housed us in a basic four bedroom, two bathroom Cape Cod. Downstairs was a beautiful finished basement and outside were a playhouse for me and an in-ground swimming pool, all of which my father built with his own hands because Pop could figure out how to make anything. Mom made sure we were well fed both physically and spiritually and clothed in the finest hand-me-downs. We were always clean. My parents perfected the art of "making do" with what they had. Mom and Dad were people in the community that others respected, sought counsel, and borrowed money from. They were the couple that pastors befriended and whose house parties others looked forward to attending. They were happily married for 44 years until the day my father died. My parents are my heroes and I am so proud to be their daughter.

Today, Mom sits quietly listening to the sounds of life around her. At ninety-two, she has short-term memory loss due to Alzheimer's/

Dementia and she is completely blind from the glaucoma she was diagnosed with in her fifties. Sadly, one of the many things that she forgets is that she can no longer see. When she awakens in the morning or in the afternoon from a nap, she must be reminded of this fact when she asks us why it so dark in the room. My sister and eldest brother and our spouses alternate caring for and housing Mom and our ninety-one-year-old stepfather who also has Dementia. Mom's face and skin, though marked with dark circles around her eyes from the eye drops she has taken daily over the years, is still beautiful. During the months she stays with my husband and me, I delight in dressing the woman who used to delight in dressing me. She often asks, "What color am I wearing today?" or "What do your friends say about how I look?" or "Where is my jewelry?" and she is sure to remind me to apply her lipstick, adding a little to her cheeks before leaving the house.

Mom once said to me many years ago when I was a teenager, "Anything really worth having in life is never easy." As difficult as it sometimes is caring for elderly parents at home, it is worth having them with us. Mom is worth it not just because she is my mother, but because of all that she is still becoming. She is still very much alive, makes her presence known, and commands the respect she has always received. At ninety-two, often seated in a wing chair or on the piano, or reclining with her graceful hands placed one on top of the other on her lap, Mom watches all of us with her gifted ears. Patiently, she listens for her cue to offer a word of advice; to give a not so gentle chastisement; or while walking her from her wheelchair, to shock you with a threat about where she might kick you if you make her fall. At night, she might render an impromptu sermon at the dinner table; whisper a risqué comment meant to intentionally produce a laugh; shimmy into bed and proclaim that indeed ALL of her body parts are working; or break into a song that she plays and sings on a piano that she can no longer see, but can feel by ear. Often she will testify that she has come this far by faith and remind you that when all is said and done, no matter how difficult things might be, God is still on the throne.

In times when she can't remember a thing and in her most lucid moments, with remarkable wit and great wisdom, she lets us know, Mother is here.

Watching Ollie through the Years

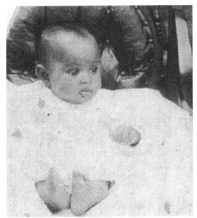

1925

Ollie (left) with sister Rene
circa 1938

Ollie and Arthur Beckett 1944

Ollie Cooking circa 1965

My Heroes circa 1968

Mom & Dad on their first cruise 1971

The Beckett Family Portrait 1980

Newly Engaged Ollie in 1993

Jumping the Broom 1993

ETHEL LEE HARRISON CLARK

Linda
Continue to learn American
culture. It's the key
to peace.
Love, Cathy T.

By: Cathy Tyler

My mother Ethel Lee Harrison Clark was born in a tin-roofed Creole cottage with weatherboard siding. The home, which is no longer standing, sat on the bank of the Bogue Falaya River on the north shore of New Orleans. The Bogue Falaya curls through St. Tammany Parish and ultimately pours out into Lake Pontchatrain. The river was named for its Choctaw natives who, like my mother's grandmother and great grandmother and their ancestors before them, lived, fished, washed clothes, bathed, and were baptized on the edge of that same river bank. Her mother married very early —long before (in the voice of my mom) "she had even become a young lady." My mother's mother and her 18-year-old husband, my grandfather, moved into that traditional Creole home facing Kemper Street. My grandmother would give birth to my mother in that cottage where my mother would live for most of her childhood.

Kemper Street in the 1920s and 30s was home to African American families who worked as domestics and laborers for wealthy New Orleans summer residents. Gray moss hung from the large oaks that lined their street which has since been renamed Lee Lane. Lee Lane is now dotted with French restaurants, pastry shops, bookstores, teahouses, and antique and bookshops. Countless hours perusing those antique shops together became a favorite mother/daughter outing when I would make my bi-annual visits during my mother's later years. Mommy loved fine linens, flowers, china, and antique photographs. As she aged, her youngest grandson found out just how much she also loved to dance to the hit song from the movie Casablanca, "As Time Goes By." I thank God we were able to capture on video that moment of her dancing in her living room with my youngest son Matthew. My son, mirroring Jay-Z and wearing sunglasses, placed a pair of sunglasses on his grandmother and called her Beyoncé, which made my dad shout from his easy chair, "Go 'head, girl!" While Alzheimer's began to steal her voice, it had also finally freed her to dance and break out into song, a pleasure that her quiet demeanor would never have sanctioned prior to that time

Flowers

Her very essence could be characterized simply by her love of flowers. It was evidenced in every memory of happiness she would share with her seven children. You could always count on any of her memories including a description of a magnolia, an azalea bush, or a gardenia. She even had my father move a gardenia bush to all three houses they lived in throughout their nearly 69 years of marriage. Not surprising, the last house where that gardenia bush landed happens to be on Gardenia Street in Abita Springs, Louisiana. She bonded with my husband Michael while planting flowers around our mailbox. My three sons never entered her front door on the first day of a trip to Louisiana without a bouquet of flowers to present to her. And my husband designed a garden dedicated to hers and my father's memory in our own backyard surrounded by azaleas, dogwood, and magnolia trees. My mother loved recounting the first time she laid eyes on my dad and telling stories of how he courted her. "We used to sit beneath a blooming magnolia tree lit up at night by the moonlight," she often recalled. She loved that man of hers who died just three weeks before she passed away in early 2017.

She first saw my dad when he had just moved to Louisiana at the age of 12. She loved recalling the moment she first laid eyes on him. "He was walking down the street and I said right then and there, I was going to marry that curly haired boy," my mom would say. As kids, we loved that story and would beg her to tell us over and over again how she met daddy. And she would rise to the occasion to let anyone within earshot hear their story.

The Wedding

On September 12, 1948 in a hurricane strength downpour that forced an outdoor wedding onto the gariere (creole porch) of her parents' home, she married Hollie James Clark—her 20-year-old curly haired, handsome groom. Her wedding day had been planned for the spring of 1949 but was moved up because of the repeated callous and emotional rage her father subjected the family to that ultimately robbed her and her siblings of a happy childhood. When asked why she chose a September wedding she explained, "I was already engaged but not planning on marrying until the spring. But one day while I was ironing a white blouse my daddy came into the room and stepped on the sleeve. When I told him he had stepped on my blouse he turned around, walked back toward me, and stepped on it again." After hearing about that encounter, my father insisted that my mom marry him immediately.

Poppa Stoppa

For years, I thought my grandfather's name was "Poppa Stoppa." The grandkids called him "Poppa Stoppa" behind his back because of his unsettling ability to stop all the fun. Our Paw Paw was the town's iceman and my grandmother, like most African American women at the time, took in ironing and was nanny to the children of a wealthy north shore family. As for my mother, a very gentle spirit, she adored her mother and feared her father who drank too much. Consequently, her childhood was filled with fear and unpredictability, to say the least. Her father had a long history of having surreptitious affairs with both women and strong drink. My mother showed no resentment to my grandfather and visited him often after escaping his den of terror.

The Value of Hard Work and a Good Education

While I am a proud first generation college graduate, my mother had only one dream as a child. She wanted to go to college and become a schoolteacher. Her dream was aborted because her attendance was often interrupted after she became the primary caregiver of her younger siblings. She began babysitting when she was only five-years-old—too young to even change the diapers of her younger sister Ruby. That task was given to her Aunt Josephine who lived across the street. Five-year-old Ethel Lee had to gather up her baby sister and toddler brother, and walk across the street to have their diapers changed several times a day while her mother and father were at work. While she could never not recall taking care of other people, her children never once heard her complain. As her siblings grew older, Ethel was able to get a job at age 10 washing dishes for a neighbor whose husband, Coach Galloway worked at the segregated white high school. The Galloways' returned home from a vacation one summer and brought back a pearl ring as a gift to my mother, the first gift she recalled not being a hand-me-down. An older schoolmate took that ring from her, which broke my mom's heart. She always talked about that ring. I believe that experience is why my mother would later tell her children, "If you can't afford it, you don't need it."

The Galloways only paid enough to take care of my mother's movie show ticket at the Star Theatre on Columbia Street and buy popcorn and a Pepsi. The zenith of her childhood years was meeting her friend Pearl at the picture show on Saturday afternoons. Pearl would eventually become my mother's sister-in-law. We teased our mom that she plotted her friendship with our Aunt Pearl to get to our dad. Her lifelong relationship with my Aunt Pearl was an exceptional example of sisterhood and friendship. Now it literally takes my breath away to read letters between the two of them from the summer of 1946, discussing summer trips, buying dresses, and meeting up on Saturday afternoons. My mother shared that on most of those Saturday afternoons her father took her dishwashing money, forced her to take her brother along to the show, and only left her with enough money to pay for both her and her brother's ticket. That left no money for the popcorn and the Pepsi she looked forward to at the show. One can only imagine that the money she earned washing all those dishes during the week was likely used to subsidize her father's weekend drinking binges. I remember sneaking moments to read from her black diary that my younger sister now keeps. Ironically, my mother's diary entries were being written at the same time Anne Frank wrote in her red and white checked diary while hiding in an attic in Amsterdam during the years of the Holocaust. Anne Frank was only one year older than my mother and like Frank, my mother used her imagination to mask her fear in the midst of chaos.

Feminism and the Church

My first cognizant memory of my mother was of me seated on her lap in church. Looking back, I now realize that was the very moment I became a feminist. A traveling minister who frequented our church was preaching a sermon about the biblical character Jezebel. This minster was the exact double of Colonel Sanders (white hat and suit), except that he was a very fair skinned African American. For years he tormented the community by walking the streets of the black neighborhoods on Saturdays and in his left hand he cracked what appeared to be a bullwhip shouting out that women who dressed in what he deemed cheap street clothes that were too tight and too colorful were wenches who needed to be saved. He ranted about loose women who wore ponytails and lipstick. I can clearly recall which hand he carried that whip in because my grandmother's house where we spent most Saturdays was on the left side of 28th Avenue. When the preacher turned the corner on our grandparents' street, like clockwork we kids would scramble onto the galleries for fear of being struck or even being kidnapped and boiled by Rev. Johnson.

I recall that on this particular Sunday morning the bullying being spewed by Rev. Johnson began to grow increasingly louder. The louder he belched out his demeaning insults about women, the quicker my mother's fingers worked to unbraid my curly hair forming two ponytails. She then took her fingers, placed them on her lips and rubbed my cheeks with her deep red lipstick. Many years later when I asked her about that day at church, in her soft voice she said, "No one determines your goodness but you." That is how my mother peacefully protested.

Years later, my mother taught me a lesson about vanity. I had a beautiful royal blue knit bikini that I am sure was a hand-me-down from someone summering on the north shore. The suit was pretty high fashion for an 11-year-old and I couldn't wait to wear it since I had just learned to swim the summer before. That same year my dad and his buddies had gotten the city to construct a swimming pool for the black community. Unfortunately, right before the summer school break began, I was walking with my older brother down our driveway lined with crepe myrtle trees that my dad and uncle kept beautifully grated with white oyster shells. We saw a couple of dogs we were not familiar with so I started to run and the dogs took chase. I tripped and slid for what seemed like 10 yards flat on my belly. Oyster shells had to be plucked out of my skin. Blood was everywhere and while the pain was unbearable, the only thing I could think to say at that moment was that I would not be able to wear my bikini that summer. Of course, my brother couldn't wait to tell my mother about my fashion disappointment. That bikini was packed away for the summer. While my mother loved me, she did not tolerate the emptiness of vanity. She was my constant reminder that "a pretty face with a conceited spirit will win you few friends."

My mother never hid her disappointment in me. She would routinely post a weekly dinner menu and dishwashing schedule to our refrigerator. I loathed doing the dishes. My dad and brother loved baseball and would watch games on television during the summer evenings if my brother wasn't playing in a league started by my dad and his friends. One evening while I was doing the dishes after dinner, I turned the television to a movie. My brother and dad walked in and without asking me, quickly switched the station to a baseball game. I protested and they ignored me. There I stood washing the very dishes that they had just eaten from. I stormed down the hallway to my bedroom and boldly announced that I was no one's "damn" slave. My dad was devastated. A short while later my mother followed me to my room and said I made my dad cry and I should go and apologize. I did. While my mother understood my argument and admired my stance of feminism, she made it clear that it was never okay to be disrespectful to my dad.

Protest

She never criticized people and didn't tolerate gossip. If she caught her daughters gossiping she would quickly say, "You don't know that to be a fact." And if we retorted with our proof of fact, she responded, "Well, everyone is not the same." Her way of saying, "It's not your business." Her business was to protect her children and her husband. My dad was well known for his civil rights activism in those days and he spent nights on rooftops or in gullies armed with a shotgun to protect a home in the community that had been threatened by the Ku Klux Klan. His work meant that his kids would be met by a burning cross at their school bus stop on more than one occasion. And when my class was finally chosen to test integration some 14 years after Brown v. Board of Education, my mother told me years later that she stood on the front porch every day filled with anxiety for an entire year hoping that I would return home unharmed. That same year she allowed me to wear my new Billy Jean King Adidas tennis shoes on the first day of school emblazoned with James Brown's famous words, "Say it Loud, I'm Black and I'm Proud."

It was extraordinarily rare that she and my dad argued in front of their children. I did, however, witness one lively disagreement between my parents. It was hurricane season so it happened during the fall. At that time my dad owned two cars. My mom was one of the few women in the community who drove a car and so she was able to run errands for family and friends or take her sister or sister-in-law shopping. On this particular day, I was playing inside the car that had been packed and ready for hurricane evacuation. I was dangling my oldest sister's underwear outside the car window because she had caused me to become upset about God knows what. There was a group of cousins and other schoolmates playing basketball next to our house in what we called the garden so I thought exposing my sister's undies was a great revenge. Suddenly, my mother stormed out of the house. I knew she was coming for me. My dad was running behind her and she had what appeared to be a steak knife in her hand. I heard her yell, "I don't want you to go!" and then stoop down out of my view. I was thinking my parents were getting a divorce because I had never witnessed them arguing until that moment. I was terrified. The year was 1964 and my dad had placed a Johnson Humphrey presidential bumper sticker on the other car. My mom was trying to remove the sticker by scraping it with the knife because she had received threats from someone on our party line. Private phone lines were a luxury in those days. My sister later told me that our mom had on a number of occasions let out the air in my dad's tires to keep him from going out in the middle of the night to fight against racist attacks.

Education

An education was so important because it was the one thing she wanted most. But while that opportunity eluded her as a child, she did not give up. She was always looking for teachable moments to define the virtues of humility, courage, and hard work. And she lived every day of her life with determination while encouraging her children to work hard in school. When I suffered college fatigue during the summer of my senior year, my mother packed my suitcase, walked me down the hallway, out the front door, and stood next to my dad's car until it was no longer in sight. She was determined that I would finish college. Years later she took that same walk with her oldest granddaughter, but this time she got into that car and drove with my sister and niece two hours to the college and helped her unpack her suitcase before leaving that campus.

Once her kids were older, she began taking night classes at a local high school and later attended evening classes at Southeastern Louisiana University while working on the weekends to clean homes or care for a weekender's small children. When I was nearing junior high school, I began to notice something strange about my mother's behavior. At the time we did not have a clothes dryer. She would do laundry in the evenings and I noticed that in the dark of night she would go out to the backyard and hang the clothes to dry on a clothesline. I saw the need to follow her one evening so that I might explain to her that I had checked the clothes on a number of mornings before heading to school and they were always still wet. I felt the need to explain to her that the sun is what dries the clothes. She paused, turned to me with one arm still extended up to the clothesline, one clothespin short of hanging my very own "Monday" blue embroidered step-ins, (her word for panties) and said to me, "Baby, I know the sun dries the clothes but I don't have time in the day to hang the clothes. I have work and school." What she didn't say but my siblings and I understood is first and foremost she had to take care of her children and husband. She was determined to achieve her education and her will defied nature itself.

She was busy taking on the care of two summer homes that belonged to a wealthy Norwegian shipping magnate whose company was based at ports in both New York and New Orleans. This job turned my mother into a Bonwit Teller, a 1960s fashion icon on Sunday mornings. The nearly new hand-me-downs were those of her employer who was always on the social pages of New York and New Orleans newspapers. Her employer could never wear the same suit twice. That would have been a horrible fashion and social gaffe.

My mother's experience working as a domestic was somewhat different from other domestics in the south. It was summer and her employer Mrs. Niels Johnsen was married to a Norwegian who had migrated from Norway in the 1920s. Racism was and still isn't a deeply embedded systemic problem in Norway. Norwegian Vikings were explorers who appreciated cultural differences around the world and brought back to Norway some of that cultural diversity. On the other hand, America's racism derived from colonialism that conquered, stole, and stayed. My mother and Mrs. Johnsen were friends who shared their love of flowers and fashion magazines. My mother would come home and say, "You know she sunbathes naked right in front of me." Mrs. Johnsen had adopted her husband's European comfort that he brought with him to south Louisiana. She also saved her *Town and Country, Vogue,* and *Harper's Bazaar* magazines for my mother to share with her girls. One day when my mother arrived at work, she was greeted by a very excited Mrs. Johnsen with an announcement. With a coupon in hand, she came into the kitchen and said, "Ethel look, this was inside this month's Vogue. There is a fashion magazine for Afro American women that's coming out and your girls need to get it!" My sister and I put our money together, $9.00 to be exact, for a full year subscription for the inaugural *Essence Magazine.*

Achievement

My mother was able to receive her education and began her multiple award winning career managing the school lunch program in St. Tammany Parish where she traveled to national conventions to be honored for her outstanding interactive nutrition program that included television character dress up week for her and her staff, faculty, and school principals that was so popular it was written about in the local paper. She would be so proud of her grandsons, who received the education she knew was so important. My son Michael (Mike) is a Georgetown University graduate and is currently the national press secretary for the Democratic National Committee in Washington, D.C. fighting voter suppression just as his grandfather did in the 1960s. Malcolm (Max), my middle son, graduated Morehouse College and Columbia University and is now attending Emory Law School. And her dance partner Matthew, (her Matt-Matt) is a Morehouse graduate and a budding screenwriter. As for me, I know that my ability to balance a family and maintain a successful career as a journalist and communications strategist is in large part the sum of the many years of watching my mother.

Her strength, courage, humility, and nurturing spirit are the virtues I continue to live by each day. Shortly before she passed away, I visited her for a week and we slept together in her bedroom. One night I whispered to her that I hoped she knew how much I loved her and how I still needed her. And while she had lost her ability to communicate verbally, she reached over, grabbed my hand, and kissed me on the forehead. I thank God every day for giving me that moment with my mother.

I only regret that I never replaced her pearl ring.

With Hollie James Clark

Ethel Lee Harrison Clark
(1930-2017)

PRECIOUS R. WOODARD

By: Janice Woodard Roberts

A story of my mother's purpose, vision, and loving sacrifice
"Even in her golden years, she continues to inspire others."

"What's in a name? That which we call a rose by any other name would smell as sweet" (Romeo and Juliet. Act I, Scene 2, 47-48)[1]. My mother's name is Precious, and she is sweeter than a rose and much more than her name. She is indeed a treasured jewel and most beloved. Her life's example has been a blessing to our family, her church family, our community, and friends. Even in her golden years, she continues to inspire others through her many acts of kindness, encouragement, faith, determination, and resiliency. Now, having the opportunity to share her story is a gift to me, and I hope it is a gift to others.

It seems like it was just yesterday, yet it was over thirty years ago. After I graduated from Clemson University with a Bachelor's of Science degree in civil engineering, I heard my mom softly weeping in a restroom stall at a McDonald's restaurant. When she came out of the stall, I asked why she was crying. She said her fervent prayer had been that God would let her live to see her children all grown up and able to take care of themselves. It was very emotional for her, for it was only one of the few times in my life that I had seen her cry. Another

---

[1] Shakespeare, William, Romeo and Juliet. The Oxford Shakespeare. 1914.

time was when she dropped me off at Clemson at the beginning of my freshman year. I suppose it was because I was the youngest of her nine children as well as the last one to attend college. What must have seemed like the climax to a lifetime of struggle had also become her special moment for tears of joy. I believe this was because her purpose, in some measure, was being fulfilled.

Though she became a single parent by the time I was five-years-old, she did not let her circumstances and situation define the future for us. My mother saw education as the pathway to a better life and she would often say, "If you have an education, you won't have to be under the feet of people." She believed that it did not matter where you came from or what you had, it was more important to think about where you were going. She was truly committed and never wavered from what she believed were the keys to success: faith in God, respect for self and others, education, hard work, honesty, integrity, and compassion. This reminds me of a well-known passage from scripture, "For surely there is an end; and thine expectation shall not be cut off" (King James Version, Holy Bible, Proverbs 23:18)[2].

Standing at five feet, three inches tall, Mom commanded respect and required that we show respect to others, especially our elders. She gave tall orders for discipline and was a stalwart for doing the right thing. She would often tell us that manners would take us further than money. Moreover, she instilled in us a sense of pride and confidence and the belief that we could do better.

As the matriarch and center of our close-knit family, she made sure that we had a firm foundation in the church. She taught us, "'Trust in the Lord with all thine heart and lean not unto thine own understanding; in all thy ways acknowledge Him and He shall direct thy paths" (Proverbs 3:5-6)[3]. Her faith and commitment to the church lead us

---

[2] *Holy Bible, King James Version.* Public Domain in United States of America.
[3] *Holy Bible, King James Version.* Public Domain in United States of America..

to being active in Sunday school, youth programs, and the choir. Through her actions and examples, we learned about caring, generosity, fairness, and being true to our word.

I have always found it fascinating to spend time with my mother to learn about her background and to better understand her drive and determination. This was often displayed in very subtle ways. Having those conversations helped me further appreciate the sacrifice, selflessness, and love she gave to each of us. She is the woman I watched, and my heart is full each time I reflect on the amazing job she did for her family.

My mother's journey was fraught with challenges. The years of her youth were during the Great Depression. She often told me about the difficult times, poverty lines, and what little opportunity she had to change her circumstances. She grew up very poor and recalled that her mother and family did not have a stable home environment. They moved what seemed to be nearly every month. She found this quite unsettling and knew she wanted a better life for herself and later for her children.

My mother would often accompany her mother to work and learned about being a maid and cook. Mom believed that sometimes her mother would take her to work just so she could get a meal for the day when they were facing hard times. It was through these experiences that she had the first opportunity to see what "a better life" looked like.

Many of the families for whom my grandmother worked had children and lovely homes. Mom was particularly fond of one family and their daughter, Carolyn, who was two years younger than my mom. They played with dolls, combed each other's hair, and enjoyed each other's company. Carolyn played the piano beautifully, and my mother admired her talent. They were from two different races and backgrounds in the Jim Crow South, and their opportunities were quite different.

By the time she was in her early teens, Mom felt like she was on her own and had to make a way for herself. At thirteen or fourteen-years-old, she was taking care of herself by working after school as a maid. She made it a practice to be punctual and dedicated. Mom often shared stories about her experiences with many families, including one where the mother of the household would often tell her to just eat her supper, head home, and not worry about working. My mom spoke about the compassion of the woman, and how grateful she was to be on her way in early dusk to arrive home before nightfall on very cold, wintry days.

In contrast, Mom also talked about the families who did not recognize her human dignity, and how some would throw away their leftover food even knowing she was in need. Moreover, there was another family who failed to pay her after she had worked all week long. Mom often talked about how she fretted when this happened, but how God always made a way.

From time to time, she reflected on these stories and used them as examples to illustrate how we can make the choice to show compassion for others as an act of kindness and to protect the human spirit. In addition, Mom would say emphatically that it is better to be compassionate for we never know when we would need someone to give us a drink of water. Moreover, she taught us the lesson about how to be resilient when staring down disappointment.

When I was eight-years-old, my mother bought a three-bedroom brick, ranch-style house across town. My brother, who was wounded in Vietnam, used his Veterans Administration loan to make the down payment. At that time, women sometimes could not secure loans for property. This was quite a step-up from our three-room wooden house with a dirt yard. I can imagine that as she reflected on her upbringing and conditions at eight-years-old versus this moment, this was a much happier occasion.

As we prepared to move to the new house, we were able to fit our life's belongings into the back of a pick-up truck; however, we were not ashamed because while my mother may have understood that we were poor in circumstances, she never spoke of this to us. Instead, she talked in hopeful terms and used encouraging words about what we could achieve and what was to come if we worked hard. She demonstrated the scripture "strength and honor are her clothing; and she shall rejoice in time to come" (Proverbs 31:25)[4].

Our new house had a large front and back yard with beautiful centipede grass, which was the perfect place for us to run and play. Mom had achieved one of her primary goals, which was to provide a better place to rear her children. I spent most of my formative years in this house and remember the continued sacrifices that she made to ensure that we had a fair chance at a better quality of life.

Mom rose early each morning, prepared breakfast for us, and left home by 6:15 a.m. to head to her job where she worked in a cafeteria as a cook. She was able to get this job because she used to iron for one of the men who worked in human resources. She would wear a bright white uniform and white shoes, which she would have polished or asked that we polish the night before. She returned home at 3:30 p.m. in the afternoon, took her daily power nap, and then prepared dinner for her family. We often marveled at her energy and stamina. On payday, she would stop by the Winn-Dixie grocery store and take a taxi home since we did not have a car. On occasion, we would meet her at the bus stop to help her carry the bags, which usually included a bag of popcorn or some small treat for us. I can remember always being excited that she was coming home.

During the holidays, she purchased boxes of fruit and nuts so that we had something in the house during the Christmas break. She also ensured that we could participate in the gift exchange with other students. This often meant giving a box of Life Saver's candy, chocolate covered cherries, or something small, but we felt good about it.

---

[4] *Holy Bible, King James Version*. Public Domain in United States of America.

I recall the time my mother learned to drive. Unbeknownst to us, she had quietly taken driving lessons. She said that she needed her independence to be able to drive herself wherever she needed to go. Shortly thereafter, she bought her first car when she was over fifty-years-old. Having her driver's license and independence would prove to be a wonderful thing. She would take others to their doctors' appointments and drive some of her friends to church. She continued to drive and demonstrated this independence until she was 87-years-old.

There are numerous lessons I learned from mom's time while she worked for over 20 years at the insurance company. On one occasion, I recall one of my sisters asking her if she had gotten tired of working in the cafeteria and if she wanted an office job. My mom responded that no one knew if she was a cook or a nurse since both wore the white uniforms. She also said that as a cook, she was making an honest living and that when she spent her dollars, they too were green and no one knew how she earned them.

Mom worked very hard and as is described in scripture, "She watches over the affairs of her household and does not eat the bread of idleness" (Proverbs 31:27)[5]. From her hands, she provided for us and did not seek public assistance; you see she believed that poverty could not only be a state of being, but more importantly, could become a permanent state of mind. She preferred the path of hard work, self-reliance, and the family helping each other.

She repeatedly touted what an education could do for us, and she walked the walk by attending night school. She regularly attended Parent and Teachers Association (PTA) meetings. When schools in the south began to integrate, she raised her hand for her children to be in the first group to integrate Olympia High School. Mom read the newspaper daily and kept abreast of current events. She always voted, and to this day, she still votes and has not missed an election since African Americans got the right to vote.

---

[5] *Holy Bible, King James Version*. Public Domain in United States of America.

Mom purchased the World Book Encyclopedias for us so that we could do research reports at home. Furthermore, my mother worked as many as three jobs at one time so that we could participate in sports, school band, cheerleading, and other extra curricula activities. And to my surprise, one Christmas Eve she made a huge sacrifice to purchase a piano for me. The joy I felt reminded me of the time she surprised my sister and me with twin banana-seat bikes, which had tassels on the handle bars and a white basket with flowers on the front.

In retrospect, I recognize how tough it must have been, yet mom wanted to see us have the best chance possible to be successful. Additionally, she wanted us to have a happy and prosperous life. She did not dwell on what we didn't have, but always seemed to find a way to make ends meet.

After I graduated from Clemson University, I began my career with AT&T (formerly BellSouth) in Metro Atlanta. Sometime thereafter, I became acquainted with one of the managers in the company. She was an older woman, but immediately made a connection with me. Later, when I was visiting my mother in Columbia, I mentioned that I had met Carolyn, who was from Columbia. As we continued the discussion and as I provided more details about Carolyn, my mom connected the dots. She believed that Carolyn was the daughter of one of the families for whom my grandmother had worked.

As it turns out, Carolyn was the same young girl who had played with my mother nearly fifty years earlier. My mother simply said, "God is good!" She knew education could take us further, but she said she never imagined that it would be to this extent. I later told Carolyn about my mother, and she couldn't believe that I was Precious' daughter. Carolyn reminisced about my grandmother's cooking and reflected on how she loved both my mother and grandmother. I swelled with pride be-cause I knew what sacrifices my mother had to make so that I could become a college graduate and go on to work in a professional job.

In 1997, mom was featured in an article in the South Carolina State newspaper with the headline "Simple lessons of self-reliance---Mother's gifts to her children still inspire others." The article was written by Christine Crumbo, and the recognition was the result of Larry Wilson, then CEO of PMSC software company, sharing my mother's story with Columbia's Chamber of Commerce and The University of South Carolina Board of Trustees. Larry met my mother when he was a college student in the late sixties and while she worked in the cafeteria at Seibels & Bruce Insurance Company. He was inspired by my mother and thought she was a real-life example for other South Carolina families. Larry said that mom dispensed advice to him, and he would later share how he admired the way she reared her family. To him, it "showed the potential of South Carolina," and he believed the state was "one generation away from having prosperity." Mom symbolized for him what every South Carolinian could achieve with an education.

Mom revealed in the article that in our earlier days, we were so poor that she had to write on the ground in the dirt outside our home to teach us. Yet she taught all of us to read before we started school. The article highlighted that she taught us more than reading and counting; she "showed us self-reliance---that we could fashion something important and whole from meager things at hand." The punch line in the article, as described by Ms. Crumbo, was that my sister, Jackie Nelson, had become a computer programmer and manager working for Larry Wilson at PMSC.

I frequently reflect on various events, such as what happened after graduation and the feature story in the newspaper and my mom's life. She demonstrated strength, intelligence, and resourcefulness. She was able to achieve her dream of nurturing her children to become productive citizens. After many years of persistent sacrifice, her children

---

[6] Crumbo, Christine, "Simple lessons of self-reliance/Mother's gifts to her children still inspire others." *The South Carolina State Newspaper*, circa 1997.

went on to have careers as a pharmacist, a civil engineer, a computer programmer, a network engineer, a teacher, a paralegal, a mail carrier, and a roofer. Additionally, her children are business executives and business owners and a retired military officer.

As Christine Crumbo wrote twenty years ago about Precious Woodard's children--- "They write not in the dust of front yards, but on computers and chalkboards," and since the article, we have sat in board rooms making decisions about businesses, just as the men in the families for whom my mother worked used to do.

Today, at 91-years-old, my mom can still be found reading the daily newspaper and working in the church; she has spent over 65 years in some capacity as church secretary, assistant secretary, choir member, and officer of the Senior and Jubilee choirs. My mother is a member of the Jubilee Choir and often sings, "Oh No, I Won't Turn Back." Giving thanks to God, she will simply say on occasion, "I'm so glad that none of my children are on the poverty line." I know that the progress we've made warms her heart. She knows that she stayed committed to her purpose.

I am grateful and blessed to have Precious R. Woodard as my mother. She is the woman I watched, experienced her love, and remembered the many stories she told about her life. Because of her, I have a rich reservoir that I tap into for strength, courage, and determination. I hope others find the same in her story.

As a tribute to my mother and for the collective gratefulness of our family, I have written the poem "The Faith of Our Mother."

The Faith of My Mother

By Janice Woodard Roberts

Dedicated to my mom, Mrs. Precious R. Woodard,
for your guidance and loving sacrifice.

I am so glad you knew your purpose
God showed you what to do
To guide, nurture and love your children
To teach us to be confident and true

You had a vision for the future
And worked hard to see it come to pass
Seeing beyond your circumstances
You believed the difficulties would not last
You did not waver from your commitment
For you had made a vow to the Lord
To teach us about Him
And to make sure He was in our heart

You taught us about learning
How important it is to give
You knew with education
It was the best path so that we could well live

I thank God for your sacrifice
I thank Him for your care
I thank you for believing
That we could do anything, if only we dare!

Precious R. Woodard

The Women We Watched

ELLA B. PARRISH

By: Kemberly Harrington

She very short in statue but very tall in love, grace, and guidance. She was the kind of person you enjoyed talking to and reasoning with. As I write a synopsis about "The Woman I Watched," it will help me to remember the time past, the days I watched, and the time ahead that portrayed the life she instilled in me.

She married the love of her life at age 18. To this union, five children were born. Beatrice, Jesse, Kemberly, Portia, and Frederick. By age 27, she had five children.

She had a different kind of love for each of her children, making each child feel particularly special as only a loving mother could.

I will take a few minutes of your time and share with you what I experienced from a woman who taught me a how to be a woman in the in our very short 19 years together.

I always thought my mama had superpowers. But now that I am older, I have come to realize that this woman I watched was human just like me.

Growing up, every night that I passed her room she was always reading her Bible or praying. Never underestimate the power of a praying woman. Sometimes I would go in my room and purposely walk out and look in her room and I would notice she would still be on her knees praying. I often wondered what she was saying to God. I knew that I had to say my prayers before bed. But I felt like I could not talk to Him for any length of time.

Not praying before bed was a no-no in our home. Your siblings would tell your parents. I was never told on. This was something that I never ever got in trouble about. This was ingrained in my soul. She taught us to pray before each meal, morning and night, and to pray when we encountered problems. The woman I watched taught me to take it to God in prayer. I wanted to pray because I watched my mama pray. I always wondered if my prayers were as meaningful as hers.

There is no doubt in my mind that mama was a precious gift from God. She had so much grace, love, and patience, the epitome of a virtuous woman (Proverbs 31:10-31). My mama taught me to walk in love and to give to those in need. Even though she had five children, she loved us equally but in different ways. It was like she knew what love we needed at that exact time and place. She treated us as individuals and made each of us feel as if we were her favorite. Not a day went by that I did not feel special or that I could have or accomplish anything I desired.

She touched my heart in so many ways with her strength and smile. She taught me to have a relationship with God and that with God all things are possible (Mathew 19:26). She inspired me to become the adult, spouse, and parent that I am today. She was a good example of a positive person. My mama taught me to push through even in the darkest times. Knowing that weeping may endure for a night but joy comes in the morning. I will forever celebrate her memory. Writing this tribute to her is with sincere gratitude, for all of her unconditional love expressed through prayer and throughout her daily activities. She taught me to always take God with me, and she taught me to stay prayed up.

As I got older, my prayers went on a little longer and became more meaningful. I began to emulate the prayers of my mother; praying for my husband, our child and other family members.

The super woman portrayed cleanliness in every area of my life. I grew up in a home with six other people. We had a comfortable three-bedroom home, with one bath, a living room, family room, kitchen, carport. After supper all dishes had to be washed and put away. Rarely was there any food left to put up unless it was a holiday. The kitchen floor had to be mopped each night. I shared dish duty with my older brother Jesse Jr. I hated washing dishes. Even to this day! We either had a week of morning shift or evening shifts.

She started with bath time around 7:00 p.m. All baths were done by 8:00 p.m. She would intentionally look at us to see if we had bathed well, and if not, we were directed back to the tub.

Each morning before school she combed my hair and my younger sister's. She did all this before leaving to go to work in the laundry room of the main hospital in Lakeland, Florida. She prepared breakfast, and made our lunches for school each day. The last thing she did after braiding my hair was putting Vaseline on my face, legs, and arms to stop the dryness and to cure ashy skin. Boy how I hated it then, but how I appreciate it now. She reminded us to brush our teeth before leaving for school.

She left for work at 6:45 a.m. She always said, "I don't want to come home to a dirty house." Therefore, we all had household chores assigned and we knew to finish them before heading to school. The woman I watched made sure that not only were her kids clean before she left, but her house would be clean when she returned from work.

She hated an odor. An odor reminded her of germs, infection, or plain old filth. The same hygiene she taught me, I used it successfully in raising my son, Brandon.

I became a missy at a very early age in life so my mama taught me to go through a routine from head to toe. You never leave home in bedroom or house slippers, wrinkled clothes, with uncombed hair, or not having brushed your teeth. Mama would say, "If you smell yourself, then someone else smells you too." We were poor, but we were always clean. The embarrassment of wearing dirty cloths and having body odor was never a label I wore or experienced. My mother made cleanliness our habit.

Having a family was my mother's greatest joy. My mama came home after working an eight-hour shift at the hospital laundry department and cooked a full dinner for her husband and children. She made home-made biscuits every day except on Fridays. It was amazing how she would feed seven people on one whole chicken. At dinner, we always sat down as a family at the table to eat. She hated when we got older and we could not make it to supper because of other obligations. Her motto was "I hate for us to be eating like cows."

Before we ate, we all had to recite a Bible verse after she blessed the food. You could only say "Jesus wept," once a week, and you can bet we kept a tally of who had said it. When we were done with saying our Bible verses, the woman I watched would then to step in our tiny world. She asked about our day and what happened at school or play. We all had to participate. It seemed liked she knew all the right answers and the right way to solve any problem. For each one of us, she listened and always made me feel that this time of the day was the best because it was shared with family.

She made me feel that my contribution to the conversation was the best. She never ever put me down or belittled me in any way. She always pointed out my strong points and things she thought would help find a solution to the problem. When I was done with my time to share I felt as if I could conquer the world. I felt that nothing was too big that it could not be handled with food and conversation with family. She had a way of making me feel special. Mama made me believe that what I contributed was not only necessary, but she let me know that she understood that I had put a lot of thought into what I was saying and that she valued it.

She enjoyed our laughter, encouraged us to eat our meal and further motivated us by telling us our reward would be syrup with biscuits. She made the best biscuits.

She wanted us to be close. She wanted all of us to be our own person within the family. She did not want us to depend on each other's strengths or merits. She wanted us to be self-reliant.

On our birthday, mama would make our favorite dessert and let us eat as much as we wanted before anyone else could have any. My favorite dessert was banana pudding. My mama would use her biggest pot she had to prepare it in. I would take all day before reaching my limit. I can still hear my little sister and brother asking her can they have some now. She would ask if I had enough yet, and I made sure it was dark outside before anyone else was allowed to have any.

My mama taught me to make my home a happy place filled with love. I learned to keep happiness in the home by doing simple and small things.

Earlier I said that a mother knows her child. To my amazement, when she passed, my sisters and brothers all found out that she secretly told each one of us that when she and my father were gone home to glory, they wanted us to let our youngest brother Fred have the family home. She felt like the four of us would be able to afford to purchase our own homes. She stressed that we should let Fred and his family have the family home.

My mama was a very respectable person. She said in order for someone to respect you, you must be a respectable person. "Respect is earned, and respect don't lie", she'd say, "Let your word be your bond". Mama wanted us to be truthful and she marveled at seeing us grow

I watched her; even on days that she had no work, she'd get up and get herself all dolled up. She loved lipstick. To this day so do I. She would tell me always give men something to wonder about. Don't show all yourself to him before you marry him. Don't let the whole town know what your body is like. In order to get respect, you must present yourself in a respectable manner.

I watched her say, "yes ma'am" and "yes, sir" to her elders and she required the same from her children. Mama believed that a person's name and reputation were very important. She explained that a simple mistake could prevent you from enjoying a lifetime of enjoyment. You always respect the name you carry.

She totally respected God's house and loved Him dearly. I remember there were these girls in our church who would bully me. They did not like me because I had long hair, dimples, and everyone liked me. I would tell my mama how the bullies treated me at church. She would listen. She knew I hated confrontation and was afraid to fight. I told her I was tired of it. Once in church, this particular girl sat behind me and repetitively hit my chair and picked at me. Before the preacher started preaching, I made a joyful noise and knocked down a couple of chairs and loudly said, "Stop bullying me." My mama instantly came and got me out of the choir and took me outside. Not one time did she chastise me; she just listened, while I repeatedly apologized.

From that day, I gained all the respect from the girls who bullied me. They learned that I might be short in statue, but bullying has no place in God's house.

A few weeks passed and I was sitting on the floor in my mama's room. She began to talk about bullying and how she hated that I had to go through that. She said people are going to dislike me a lot of times because they are not happy with themselves, and that that's okay. She said, the only problem she had with this situation was that I felt the need to apologize for the many good qualities that God gave me. She told me to rejoice in my blessings. This was the first time I ever heard her say this to me. She said, "You are a beautiful black girl. Women will be jealous of you. Your job is to give them something good and wholesome to talk about. Walk and talk with pride. Don't ever stoop to your enemy's level." The woman I watched said this entire incident was based on mere jealousy.

The woman I watched taught me right from wrong. She taught me to follow the rules. Rules are to be followed personally, socially, and professionally. Mama was a person who believed in being on time. If you were to be at work at 7:00 a.m. don't get there at 6:59 a.m. Allow time for yourself before getting your day started. She stated that you should have a few minutes to spend with God before starting your day.

Rules are to be followed. She often said if you don't want to follow the rules or do what you're supposed to do, then get your own business. This way you don't have to follow the rules.

Humble yourself on your job. She stated, "Our God teaches us to be humble. If you are there to work, WORK. Do not be so quick to anger." The woman I watched displayed every day as if she was a millionaire. She said never let your left hand know what your right is doing. Don't rob Peter to pay Paul. Never be boastful. A person can tell how you are by just looking at you. Action speaks louder than words. You be in charge of letting your audience know how much you want them to know. Let your outward appearance speak volumes into your inner soul to reveal the you that you want to be. Be the best in everything you try to do. This way you know you have done all you can do. She stressed that a piece of a job is better than no job at all.

I remember when I started first grade...I was a dropout in kindergarten due to financial reasons. I was voted to be the leader of my reading group. For some reason, I was the best reader even though I only attended kindergarten for a couple of months. When my teacher, Mrs. Sanders, who lived a few houses from me, observed that each day she called my group to the front, I would start to cry. This went on for about two weeks. I remembered seeing her speaking to my mama a few days earlier. I had told my mama I did not like being the group leader and the best in the group. I told her most of the kids in class knew each other. I just want to be the best, but not a leader right now. This time before Ms. Sanders called my group, she told me to go to bathroom and wash my face. I had begun to cry because I knew it was close to my group being called to read. When I got back, another girl in class was the group leader. I was happy. I did not want to bring attention to myself. However, I was still the best reader.

When I got home, I told my mama what had happened. She asked me how did I feel about it? I told her I felt good, because I felt sad and thought everyone knew more than me because I was kindergarten dropout. Mama said, "In everything you do, be your best and do your best." I told her I was still top reader. My mama just smiled.

I remember our Sunday school teacher quit coming to church, and my Mama became my Sunday school teacher. I never heard my mama read. We always read to her. One Sunday in class she began to read. My peers began to snicker and the bullies laughed out loud. I was hurt and embarrassed. Mama was hurt and she was especially hurt because I had to experience this.

When I got home, she asked if I could help her to read better. Mama had to work the fields at an early age picking cotton, and she did not get to go to school. She married to get away from the fields. That Sunday was the last time she was our teacher. I told her I'd be glad to help her. I think she wanted to prove to my friends and me that learning never stops. Another motto that she always used was, "A quitter never wins."

The introduction to the Sunday school lesson was read out loud each Sunday by a member of the church before we all adjourned to our respective classes. The introduction was what she told me she wanted to read. I said okay. I think she wanted to prove to my friends and me that she could read. We would begin practicing reading the Sunday school introduction each Saturday evening in preparation for Sunday school. I first made sure she knew all the words and their meanings. I made sure she knew to stop at a period and pause at a coma, and show expressions as needed. The introduction never had more than three paragraphs.

Mama read like a second grader by pointing at each word and calling them out. I told her to stop pointing and to let her eyes move from word to word. We would practice every day until that Sunday. If I felt like she was not ready, I would say wait until next Sunday. I can remember seeing the disappointment in her eyes. Then she would try to reassure me that she was ready.

She was like a sponge ready to soak anything up. A couple of Sundays passed and mama was ready. Before the superintendent could ask someone to read the introduction to the Sunday school lesson, she was standing up saying the title. She did not point. She stopped at periods and paused at commas. Each word was pronounced correctly. When she was done we looked at each other and gave a big proud smile. I was proud of my mama. She read the introduction for the next several Sundays. I told her to give someone else the chance to read it. We both laughed. Mama knew that my bullies would stop picking at me because she could read.

She earned her respect by learning to read. I learned to respect her more by seeing her prove to me that you can do anything you wanted to do. Respect starts within. If you don't respect yourself, don't ask anyone else to respect you either.

She was like a sponge in education. She wanted to suck it up in one big gulp. She completed the ninth grade in night school successfully. I remembered when she was learning subject and verb agreement. I was trying to figure out a way to teach this to her so she could understand. Out of the blue she said, "she and it does and everything else do." I marveled at how her wisdom in learning was broken down so even a child could learn and understand. It was the mother in her that made this agreement in subject and verb agreement so simple.

The woman I watched told me to get a college education. She said any accredited college is okay. She always said, "Don't be like me." She said again, "A quitter never wins." I had two older siblings who had already completed college. She told me don't go through any embarrassment by putting everything in front of my obtaining a degree and reaching my goals. She said if I did not get a degree, it would be hard for me to put up with my older brother and sister. I told her I wanted to work and get a car and then go to school. She said that comes after I receive my degree. She did not want me to marry or start a family before I had a college education. Due to the utmost respect I had for this woman, even though she had gone home to be with the Lord, nothing came before me obtaining a college degree. I waited until this task was completed.

Patience

I watched this woman so patiently put one foot in front of the other. She always said, "Don't be so swift to get in a hurry with life. Life is a chance." I was the type who wanted things now. I did not want to wait. She quoted from the Bible, "Those that wait on the Lord shall renew their strength." I asked her what did she mean? She stated there is a time and place for everything. Be patient and do what you are meant to do, it will happen.

My season is not here yet. I am growing to be a leader for the next person. I watched this woman endure a lot of things, kind and unkind. I hope she knew that she set a foundation that educated five children. I hope she realized that even though she left my life when I was only 19, that she taught me to be patient and to weigh things out; that she provided guidance in decision making and instilled in me a lifetime of lessons.

She taught me to have faith in God. I told you earlier that anytime I had a problem, she taught me to take it to God in prayer.

When I would tell her my problem and she could not readily come up with an answer, she always told me to take it to God in prayer. I would say that I had. Her reply would be, "Why are you still worried about it?"

I remembered when I was growing up around Easter time. My parents always depended on their income tax check to get our Easter outfits. I always worried if the check would make it there on time. It never failed. Mama did not worry. The check was always there the Saturday before Easter. I would ask my mama if she thought the check would arrive so we could get our Easter stuff. Her reply was always, "You got to believe without any doubt."

When I found out from my oldest brother that there was no Santa Claus, I was hurt. I went to my mama and asked her. Mama said, "Now all the playful fun is out of it for you. This teaches us to believe without doubt. To believe is to have faith." Mama was a faithful woman.

I taught my child this lesson when he was seven-years-old. He always knew that Santa Claus was his parents. I taught him to believe and trust in his parents and trust in God. I taught him most importantly to pray without doubt.

My son, Brandon wanted a BMX bicycle for Christmas. It was a little high for us at that time along with all the other stuff he wanted. He had gone with me to look at one. He did not know at that time the bike started in the low 250s. He said, "Mom, that is too much." I told him to pray and believe. If it is meant to happen, it will. I told him that his dad and I would also pray about it. Christmas morning the bike was not under the tree. This was the gift he really wanted. My husband went to the garage and brought his BMX into the house. He looked at me and said, "Ma I believe." I told him all things are possible if you only believe.

I remember when I was getting ready to graduate high school. The counselor made an appointment for each student to see her for advisement on careers. When it was my turn to visit, she told me that she thought I would make an excellent checker at a small store. I said okay. This woman showed me not one grade that indicated these things to her. When I got home, I told my mama what she had said. My mama asked me how did she know me. I said she was the counselor. Mama said, "I served a higher counselor than she will ever be. You can be whatever you want to. You are number 83 out of a class of 586. You are an honor student. You have two four-year academic scholarships one from Dillard University and one from Tuskegee Institute, now Tuskegee University. You believe in God don't you? We'll let him show her."

When I went off to college, I was 17-years-old. I graduated on a Thursday and that Sunday morning my parents and my oldest sister and I were on our way to Tuskegee, Alabama. When I got there, I began to cry after my mama unpacked all my clothes. My dad asked if I wanted to go back home. I looked at my mama and she shook her head and said no. I then said no. She had taught me if I were lonely, to look to God. She had taught me to take care of myself. She left me with no worry on her face. She felt very confident that this was the place for me. She told me in everything I do to keep God first. She told me to pray. She taught me to have faith without any doubt. She taught me to respect and honor my elders. She taught me right from wrong. She taught me how to be a young lady and what things would be expected of me. She was very confident in her teaching.

I was alone and a long way from home. I had a meal card. I met people from all over the world. I remembered my mama told me to pray when I got homesick. I always prayed. I had someone sleeping on the other side of the room that I knew nothing about. I realized that God was the comforter she talked about. When months went by and no money was coming from home, I remembered what she said. Don't let your right hand know what your left hand is doing. Therefore, no one knew how broke I was. I ate on my meal card. I did not like what they served, but I ate it anyway. There were times she would send me two dollars in an envelope. She would write a letter telling me to keep myself up and study and pray. When I called home, which was very infrequently, the call was rushed but the conversation was amazing. She had a way of making me feel as she did when I was little; everything was going to be all right.

On April 7, 1973, God told my mama to come and take her rest. She had cloned this model for me to be guided throughout my life. All that I am is because of her.

This was a very sad day for me. I did not know how to respond. I remembered that she had given me all the tools needed and prepared me for her death. She often said, "We all are going to die." I felt that she was pleased with the lady I had become. She knew if I imitated this model of a woman she was, she could rest in heavenly peace. She passed away with dignity and grace.

It was spring break , my junior year of college and I decided I would stay on campus to work and make some much needed extra money. I knew my parents didn't really have the money to bring me home for the break so I called my mother to tell her I would not be coming home. I recalled that she was not feeling well the last time we spoke by phone, so you can only imagine how I felt when during my call to her I realized that she believed that I was at home with her. At that point, I decided to go home to Lakeland, Florida. When I got there, there were times she never knew who I was. I reached out to my oldest sister, and she came home the next day. We made an appointment with a specialist and he saw us the same day. The specialist called us that evening and told us to bring her to the hospital. She had a type of cancer that they had not seen before. The origin was never found.

My oldest sister was very upset and asked me to dress mama. My mama had at least five or six wigs. I pulled out her best one. In her good mind, she told me, "No, put that one back and save it for a special occasion." She was still teaching me even on her deathbed. I put it back. That was the one we put on her body for her burial.

Her first night in the hospital she hugged each of us for at least a minute. It was like she was saying her goodbye. As this strong woman hugged me, I could not imagine my life without her. I knew she needed me to take the leadership role and be strong for my siblings. That first night I stayed with her all night and it was like I could feel the cancer growing in her nose and mouth. I felt her weakness and tears saying, "I am tired. I want to go home but I hate to leave you all. I have taught you all I know. Let me go and be examples for all the world to see." She smiled at me as if it gave her joy. As I bathed her that morning and saw the cancer all over her body, she began to cry. We hugged each other, and just like she told me when I cried on her lap, I said, "It is okay mama."

I held her and told her, "It is okay, Mama. It is okay."

Watching her as she stood at the brink of life and death, I observed her saying in her own way, "I hate to leave now, but my time is up. I hope I have impacted your life like no other woman ever will. I wish I could be there to comfort you in the days coming ahead. I hope I was a good mother and prepared you for life's ups and downs. One day I hope you have a family and you take the values with you that I have tried to show and teach you. I hope you remember to always keep God first in your life. Remember it is okay for people not to like you. Just think about the many people who did not like Jesus Christ. Don't judge others unless you are perfect. Respect your elders. Remember there is no place like home. Pray, pray, and pray. Never give up. Be a godly woman. Give happily and with joy. Remember you will never be alone. I will be your angel watching over you and guiding you until we meet again. I know you don't understand why I must go, but my time is near, my sweet love one."

I could not cry as I watched her in between the two worlds. All I could think of was how this woman I watched had prepared me for this time in her own way. I thought about the bond that she had with each one of her children. I thought about how she would no longer have to stress each day how tired she was. I held her closely while she cried. I could not cry. The child that she knew as her most sensitive child was prepared. I wanted her to know that even though she was leaving me at an early age in my life, the work she had done to prepare me was sufficient. The pattern was a piece of cloth well designed.

Because of the roots she set for me, to this day, I have not been able to call another woman "Mama."

We never told her she had cancer. But Mama knew. She said her goodbyes to all of us while she was in her right mind. I felt her love. I am living her love each day. I wish I could hold her hand as she held mine. I wish I could wipe her tears away as she did mine. I wish I could smile at her as she did with me and knew everything would be all right.

I remember her saying, "Don't feel pressured to be perfect when we go to church so that people will think well of us." She said a church is like a home. A healthy home and church are places where we can let our hair down and not hide our flaws behind a façade of perfection. We should be able to reveal our weaknesses to find strength rather than conceal our faults to appear strong.

I could not understand then the way she tried to put it in words to relate to me as I do now. When she stressed worship to me, I got it that worship doesn't involve behaving as if nothing is wrong; it's making sure everything is right, right with God and with one another.

I thought about how Mama would spend an hour or two straightening my hair only for me to put it in a ponytail after she was done. I remembered her asking me why I don't wear my hair down. I told her that Mischa, my boyfriend, did not like it down. She told me to always look my best. She said when our greatest fear is letting down our hair; perhaps our greatest sin is keeping it up. It was only at that time I realized exactly what she was trying to tell me.

I felt she questioned why she was leaving so young. But she would constantly say she did not want to die before her kids could take care of themselves. She always broke it down further by explaining, "I don't want to leave any babies." All five of her children could take care of themselves. In other words, she did not leave any babies. She said that her mother left younger sisters and brothers. I watched my mama take care of her younger sisters and the one brother that lived with us. I watched her accept them just the way they were. They ate as much as we did. She never acted as if it bothered her at all. We all piled in bed and slept as if we had plenty of room. We always had plenty of food. She was never the type of person to complain. She made do with what she had; a lesson well taught.

I thought about how every day of our short time together, she prepared me to be a woman, a wife, and a mother. I looked at each one of her five children and can readily see her accomplishments. I can see her beauty, loyalty, honesty, and love.

My heart still grieves to this day for her warmth and touch. I don't cry like I used to. I smile and I say what a job well done. Through everything I have accomplished in this world, my mama was my example of this model. God, I thank you for blessing me with a role model that followed your principles. I thank you for giving me a praying woman.

I know if I were the one passing out crowns to a lady that taught me a lifetime of experiences, I'd choose my mama, Sweet Ella B. There is no woman fit enough to wear the crown as Kem's mama. I have written this poem to sum up this special lady that I watched. Mama, I modeled after you.

My mama was short in stature and she meant all the world to me.

She was sweet, respected, loving, and clean.

There was nothing about her that was mean.

Mama respected others like she wanted to be.

She prayed for her children to be all they could be.

As she exposed her children to a world that the scope of

her knowledge could not see.

She stayed on bended knee to set an example for her children to see

That without God where will they be?

Her smile was flawless, kind-hearted, and sweet

I learned to love from a lady that was so meek.

I love you. I love you.

Oh yes I do.

No one will ever take your place in my heart

You are my sweet

My sweet Ella B.

Kemberly L. Harrington

Ella B. Parrish - 1969

Ella B. Parrish
(1931-1937)

MERTIS JEAN MARIE HAWKINS PARKER

By: Reggie Tuggle

On December 17, 1927 on an isolated farm in Guthrie, Oklahoma, John and Julia Hawkins gave birth to my mother and named her Mertis Jean Marie. She was one of eleven children born to these parents. There are several words that can come close to characterizing my mother's personality: lively, smart, friendly, tenacious, humorous, but the one word that best describes her is "tough." She was tough. She came from a tough mother and she inherited the DNA "tough" gene in spades. I suspect that this trait is common among African American mothers as part of the survival instinct required to perform their role as mother as well as father and sole breadwinner in many instances. I'll speak more about the other characteristics later, but none of them will surpass her toughness.

I'm often asked how I came to be born in Denver, Colorado where there are so few African Americans; fewer then when I was born in 1947. It's a good question and I love to tell the story of how that happened. On a road trip in 1941, my grandmother, Julia, was nearly killed in a car accident. In fact, she was declared dead and taken to the city morgue. While on a slab, covered with a white sheet, her arm slipped out from under the cover and an attendant saw her finger move and called out "she's not dead." They hurried her upstairs where she got emergency treatment. She spent several months in the hospital and many more months after that recovering from her extensive injuries. My grandfather, whom I never knew, simply stayed by her side and decided to stay in Denver where I would be born five years later. To this day, I wonder if my grandmother would have received quicker and more appropriate medical care had she not been black. Who knows? My grandmother finally recovered and went on to live until she was 74. As I said, she was tough. There are other examples of her resilience, but I think this sets the stage for how my mother was nurtured.

I remember visiting my grandmother when I was about six or seven-years-old. She was the building supervisor for a boarding house. On this particular day, I went with her to the basement where the huge coal fired furnace was located. I would watch my grandmother put on a large black apron, a dirty gray scarf, and a pair of gloves and then she'd start shoveling coal. She would hum as she worked and every now and then she'd pause, take a handkerchief, and wipe sweat from her brow and shout, "Help me, Lord. Thank ya, Jesus." Then she'd return to her work. I'd try to help by picking up a piece of coal and throwing it into the furnace and she'd say, "That's it, son, just chuck that old rock in the fire." Although she had only a third grade education, she was feisty. She never let her short stature be a reason for her not to speak her mind or slap you down if you sassed her. She didn't have an extensive wardrobe. She wore just about the same dress to church every Sunday. She never owned a car and never drove one. Material things just didn't seem to matter to her. I guess the same can be said of my mother.

After graduating from high school, my mother moved the two of us into an attic apartment. That's where we lived for the first nine years of my life. It was a small two-room apartment with a tiny bathroom having only a toilet and sink where we'd go to "wash up." We didn't have a bathtub or a shower; we just did the best we could. It wasn't as bad as it may seem. Our kitchen was located two floors down in the basement. It consisted of a hot plate, a small table, and two chairs. We didn't have a refrigerator and our sink was the same sink used by the washing machine to collect expelled water between rinse cycles. Nevertheless, my mother prepared some of the best meals one could ever have; fried chicken, pan-fried cornbread, collard greens, beans, and more. Our meals were a gastronomic feast. We'd laugh and we'd talk. My mother was one of the great storytellers of all time. Later in life, I remember her being the center of attention at family reunions when it came to storytelling time. She'd mesmerize her listeners and when finished, there would be pleading requests for more; "Tell us another story, Mertis, please." She would always find another story or event to pass along. It wasn't just a story, it was her facial expressions, her acting it out, her sense of gravitas for serious issues, and humor for those meant to be funny. Her timing was impeccable and that's the key to good storytelling, the timing. More about that later.

Although for the first nine years my life I had no father in the home, I never felt unloved, never went to bed hungry, and never felt sorry for myself. We had no car so we had to walk just about everywhere, or take a bus, or have someone with a car transport us. Times were hard I think, but I didn't feel as though they were hard. We were poor, but just about all my friends were as poor as we were. I didn't realize how poor we were until my early twenties I found a box of old pictures of me and my friends as children and we looked pretty shabby, even in the photos. But we didn't feel poor and didn't act poor. Poverty is as much a state of mind as it is a state of the purse, maybe more so. In fact, my mother would often say that it isn't what one wears on the outside of the body that matters, but what's in the heart on the inside that counts. I can honestly say that for the most part I had a pretty happy childhood.

When playing outside, my mother had a simple rule. "Son, you can play anywhere outside you want so long as you can hear my voice when I call your name. If you can't hear me when I call, you're too far away from the house." I heard that speech dozens of times. And the rule was when my name was called I had to come running, not walking. If my mother had to wait too long for me to come it was a blatant act of disrespect that would not go unchallenged.

I remember a time when playing baseball in a vacant field near our house when my mother called. I could always tell generally what she wanted by how she called my name. "Reggie" was safe. It was something minor. What I never wanted to hear was "Reginald." When I heard that call I knew that I was in some kind of trouble or something. Either way I had to come running.

I was at bat one day and a pitch was in mid-flight when I heard my name, "Reggie." I dropped the bat and went running home. Climbing up the stairs and out of breath, I could barely get the question out, "Yeah, mother. What do you want?"

"Oh, I don't want anything. I just want to talk." (I said to myself, not out loud to her, "TALK. You just want to TALK.") "What were you doing," she'd ask.

"I am playing baseball with some friends," I'd reply.

"What friends are you playing with," she'd continue. Then I had to go around all the positions on the field and tell her who was playing what position. "And what position were you playing," she'd say.

I said, "I was at bat about to swing at the ball when you called my name. I came as fast as I could."

She'd be ironing or doing something about the apartment and she'd ask about school, my teachers, who was my best friend, did my shoes fit okay, and did my feet hurt. Then, without any warning or notice, the conversation would subtly shift to what happened on her job and how she hated it. At that time she worked at a local cleaners pressing clothes. The technology in those days was quite primitive compared to now. At that time, the pressing machine was huge. One placed a shirt or a pair of pants on the bottom and then pulled down a large heavy top covered with some kind of silver material onto the item of clothing and a big puff of steam would fly out all sides as it made the item as smooth and wrinkle-free as one could possibly imagine. At the end of the day, her hair was a fright, her skin oily, and her arms as thin as a rail.

She'd often say, "One day, son we're going to get a bigger and better place to live in." That day came when she passed a civil service test qualifying her to be a clerk typist for the Air Force from which she retired after more than 35 years of faithful service.

We talked about so many things: politics, church, the pastor's sermon, Jesus, my grandmother, my future plans when I got to be a man, how to manage money, why it's important to be kind, and much, much more. "Politeness," she'd say, "is a passport around the world." Looking back to those years they were some of the best in my life. It was a boy having a conversation with his mother and a mother talking to her son: not scolding, or yelling, or lecturing, just talking and getting into each other's head; exploring future options, listening to our frustrations and celebrating our hopes. The things my mother taught me still serve me to this day. I can unequivocally say that I am the man I am because of what I learned at her feet. I am convinced that one of the missing qualities in many of our families today is that parents and children don't spend time talking and sharing life experiences, learning from each other and growing together inter-generationally.

During my senior year as I was preparing to go off to college, I remember thinking to myself, *I wonder when mother is going to give me the going-off-to-college lecture.* I waited and waited and wondered when she was going to do it. I know she had something to say to me. Finally, on the way to the Greyhound bus station to catch the bus for college, I thought, *This is going to be the moment when I hear it.* We got to the bus station and still no lecture on what to do or how to behave. She was quiet all the way to the station. She helped me get my trunk out of the car and we walked over to the bus. She gave me a tight hug, and just as I was about to get onto the bus, the lecture came: "Son, never forget who you are." Those six word conveyed eighteen years of sitting at her feet; eighteen years of listening to her wisdom and her stories and watching how she handled the various situations in her own life; eighteen years of her telling me what she expects of me as a human being; eighteen years of having my values and spirituality shaped and developed; my sense of self, my dreams, and my hopes and more, all summed up in those six words, "Son, never forget who you are." Of all of the people in life that I would not want to disappoint, the most important person that comes to mind first is my mother.

While I ended up attending three undergraduate schools and three graduate schools, I began my college career at Bishop College, a HBCU institution, in Dallas, Texas. We had no money for college. During all my years in college I remember getting only $100 from home. My mother just didn't have it and I didn't ask. But every birthday she made and sent me my favorite cake (German chocolate) meticulously wrapped. I'd share it, of course, with my roommate and others. She mailed me letters on a regular basis and through them our conversations continued. I had a scholarship that paid for tuition and most of my room and board, but for spending money I'd go down to the parking lot on some Saturdays and wash the cars of other students for a few bucks. Even as sophomore class president, I was not too proud to wash the cars of other students. Every now and then someone would say in a kidding way, "Hey, slave when you get through washing that car, you can wash mine." I'd tell them for $5 I'd wash anybody's car. I always found a way to earn money. I was a furniture mover, bookstore clerk, church youth leader, and other jobs. I owe my self-motivation and self-determined nature to my mother.

I've been a pastor for nearly 46 years altogether and preaching since the age of 16. My mother never encouraged me to go into the ministry, oddly enough. I remember one day when her sister, aunt Geneva, was visiting and she asked me what I planned to do when I finished college, I told her I was going to be a preacher.

My mother stopped in mid stride and said, "A preacher, a preacher," in total incredulity.

My aunt was surprised. "Mertis, you going let that boy of yours with that good brain be a preacher?"

My mother's reaction was, "I ain't got nothing to do with that. That's between Reggie and God." My mother never discouraged me from becoming a preacher, she just never pushed it. But once the decision was announced, she was 100% behind it. In fact, she became the president of my fan club and chairperson of the prayer warrior council on my behalf. I can't remember ever missing a day in church on Sunday. We walked to church when I was a child. There was Sunday school at 9:30, followed by 11 a.m. service; frequently, we had a 4:00 p.m. service followed by Baptist Training Union (BTU), and a 7:30 p.m. service. This is what it was like virtually every Sunday, a very long and often boring and tedious day. To this day, I don't think I've missed more than 10 or 15 Sunday services in my entire life.

I was always a pretty good student, not the best, but pretty much always near the top of my class. Mother encouraged me to read as much as possible early in life. I remember reading the encyclopedia from A to Z just for the fun of it. I loved learning. I became the twin brother of Curious George, the celebrated cartoon character who was forever curious about everything. As was expected, when I made a grade less than an A, we'd have a conversation, not a lecture or a scolding, but a conversation. Why did I make a C or B? Did I do my best? Was the subject too hard? Was the teacher a good teacher? Was I paying attention? What's wrong with you, son? Was there anything she could do to help? I didn't always make A's but they were expected and I felt no loss of love from her when I made less.

Now I did mess up a few times in my childhood, and boy did I get it. Today, I think my mother would have been arrested and placed into anger management counseling or something for the way she "abused" me. I never got a spanking. No, when it came to capital punishment it came with an extension cord, and yes it made welts and sometimes drew a little blood across my behind. But what I hated almost as much as the whipp'n was the long and sometimes tiresome lecture that always followed.

She'd begin by asking, "Do you know why I whipped you?" Now this is a trick question, I soon came to discover. If I said, yes, then I had to repeat word for word what I did wrong. I had to take responsibility for my actions. If I said yes, it meant that I had the wrong attitude about what she was trying to teach me. I was acting man-ish and needed an attitude adjustment, that is, a whipp'n. If I said no that I didn't know why she was whipp'n me, she would remind me what she said and ask me if I remembered any of it. If I said I forgot then she'd say maybe more of these whipp'ns would be necessary in the future so I wouldn't forget. After the long lecture came a big hug and the words, "you know that I love you, don't you?"

I would always say, "Yes, and I'm sorry for messing up and disobeying you." She reminded me that life is tough and that I had to be prepared for any eventuality. Sour comes with the sweet, but you'll have more sweet if you avoid the sour. It's not where you've been in life that counts the most she'd say, but where you're going and with whom and with what. If I have the right attitude about the good things in life then the wrong things in life will most likely leave me alone. The crowd and your friends may not always be there to help you as you travel on your journey, but your attitude and focus will be your constant companions. Never, never, never be a follower just for the sake of following. If it feels right do it, if it feels wrong, don't. The world doesn't owe you anything. If you get anything in life it's because you've got to go out and get it. Believe in yourself. You can do anything God places in your path. She got me involved in Little League baseball and the Mile High Boys Band where I played the clarinet and was a running back on the football team. I spent seven years in scouting: Cub Scout, Boy Scout, and Explorer Scout in high school and ran sprint events on the college track team.

When I was nine, my mother got married. We moved from a little attic apartment into a house. My stepfather and I were never close and, within a year of their marriage, his true nature began to show. He was a church usher for a short time, but soon he began to drink too much and then the physical attacks and violence began to appear. When he drank, he became argumentative and belligerent. My mother became a battered spouse. Weekends were especially scary. We just didn't know what to expect when he came home and often our fears were justified. I remember having a fistfight with my stepfather when I was a high school senior. When I was 14, he killed a man in barroom brawl. I don't remember having a happy Christmas after the age of 10.

During my middle year in seminary I called home one night to speak to mother. My sister answered the phone and told me that mother was at choir rehearsal, but there was something in her voice, a timid hesitation, that conveyed to me that something was terribly wrong. When I called back the next morning before she would be going to work, my sister again answered the phone and in tears told me that mother was in the hospital with substantial injuries, broken ribs, a busted nose, etc. When I finally reached mother she told me that my stepfather had beaten her. I told her I'd take care of it. She made me promise not to come from New York to see her because she knew that I was going to kill him and that was exactly my plan. I knew where my stepfather hung out. I could fly to Denver, find, and kill him, then fly back to New York before anyone knew. In those years one could pay cash for a plane ticket and fly under any name without identification. I figured who would suspect a seminary student living in New York of murdering someone in Denver? My mother begged and later got me to promise that I wouldn't go to Denver to visit her. "I don't want you to ruin your life over a decision I made to marry him." I didn't go, but for a long time hate filled my heart. When she got out of the hospital, she carried a loaded .38 caliber gun on her at all times. He never struck her again, but she told me that she was ready for him just in case he tried. I knew she would have done it. My mother was tough.

She'd say to me more times than I can remember, "Leave him to heaven. Get on with your life."

I began looking for my biological father when I was 18-years-old. Mother never talked too much about him, claiming she didn't know a lot about his past. They met in their late teens. She became pregnant with me at age 18 and I was born the following year. I looked diligently for my father for years; finally in 1985 I retained the services of a private investigator in Freeport, New York and he found my dad on April 19, 2015 living in Detroit, Michigan. She would ask me every now and then how my search was coming along for my dad and I'd tell her the status. She'd say, "I sure hope you find your dad before I die." She had cancer and was given six months to live, but by God's grace was allowed to live another six years. She never expressed any disdain for my dad even though he left her and me without notice and didn't tell her where he was going. We had a hard time growing up but she didn't complain. I complained because I thought I was missing out on having a dad and what that meant: not going to baseball games, or going fishing, or learning how to work on a car, or doing home repairs around the house, and more. I never looked forward to the annual "father-son" day at school. I never got a birthday or Christmas gift from Dad.

When I told my mother in April 2005 (I was 58-years-old) that I had found my dad living in Detroit she seemed almost as excited as I was. "Good," she said, "praise God that after all of these years God blessed you to finally find your dad and get to know him."

My dad and I were successful in establishing a very loving and solid relationship before he passed on to glory nine months after my mother's passing. She said to me, "See how God has blessed you. You've earned three degrees, a bachelor's degree, two master's degrees, and all the work on a Ph. D. except your dissertation from Yale University.

You've been blessed to serve a loving and growing church, two wonderful daughters, and a devoted wife. You've traveled the world and been a help to countless people. Your father left you, but God's hand held you close and his blessings flowed in abundance into your life. You were blessed, son, in spite of your father's absence. His leaving us wasn't our loss, but his."

My mother was a very tolerant person, generally speaking. However, she had little tolerance for people, who lied, were lazy, and who disrespected others. I never saw her drink alcohol or smoke cigarettes or curse. But there was one four-letter word that, when she used it, one knew she had reached her last nerve. She'd say, "Ah, shit now." When that expression came out of her mouth she was vexed to the nth degree. Shut up and pay attention. Things were about to explode. That sense of passion extended to social and political issues, too. During the civil rights struggle, she encouraged me to participate in marches and demonstrations. When I was a high school senior I drove from Denver to Atlanta with two other friends, a distance of nearly 1200 miles to participate in a national civil rights march in 1964. I was only 17 but she knew that it was critical for black folk to stand up against racism and social injustice. Before leaving that night to drive there we gathered in the kitchen to pray for my safe return. We prayed often in our house. In fact, she'd remind me over and over again to put God first in all that I did. Trust God first and last.

She rarely gave out compliments when it came to one's behavior, but I came to know her highest compliment for anyone, man or woman. She'd say, "He's (She's) a decent man/women." That was it, decent. I don't know where she got that word from, but it's a powerful word. It means a person of integrity: honorable, fair, and respectful. She was something of a wordsmith. With only a high school education, she could solve most crossword puzzles because of her extensive vocabulary. She had stacks of crossword puzzles all around the house. She loved words and loved to read. Somewhere in her journey the word "decent" became very important to her and it has become very important to me. I want to be and I strive to be a decent man: decent for myself, for the Lord I serve, for my children, for my wife, for my friends, for anyone who knows me. If one wasn't decent, she'd still give you the time of day, but that's all.

My mother wasn't particularly religious, but she had a strong and profound faith. On one of my frequent visits to Denver to see her during her travails with cancer, I remember praying. One particular occasion I was compelled by the Holy Spirit to anoint her with oil and pray for her. Then she anointed me as I knelt at her feet. It was a blessed moment of intense spiritual joy that I shall never forget. We both cried as we held each other. All the same, I was surprised and later humbled by a point in my prayer for her that she interrupted me. I was praying that God would restore her health and grant her a long life. She stopped me in mid prayer and said, "Stop it. Don't pray that prayer. You gone to meddln' in God's business. Only God determines how long any of us will be here. Longevity is His domain alone. You can pray that God restores my health and heals my body, but not a longer life. Only God knows that. Leave that to Him." I was struck by the theological correctness of this understanding of life and God's grace. God has numbered all of our days even before one of them comes to be (Psalms 139).

My mother never told me what she wanted me to be when I became a man. She never encouraged me to be anything in particular. Just be a decent man that God can use to His glory. I've been blessed in life with many wonderful opportunities and done lots of things. I attended three undergraduate schools and three graduate schools; traveled to 44 countries; baptized hundreds of people including dozens of believers in the Jordan River in Israel; served as an adjunct professor at New Haven University, served on the late congressman Adam Clayton Powell's staff, pastor of a Presbyterian church for 38 years (seeing it grow from fewer than 40 members to more than 1000), first president of the Urban League of Long Island, Chief of Staff of the highest elected official of our municipal government, Director of Public Affairs of *Newsday* for 15 years (a major daily newspaper on Long Island), associate vice president of a community college for 17 years, built several houses and owned three at various times including a 42-unit apartment building in Brooklyn, president of several non-profit organizations, served on many local and national boards, the recipient of more than 300 awards, having a street named after me, and father of two wonderful and brilliant daughters (one a surgeon and the other a marketing executive for a major retail chain store).

When my wife died more than 25 years ago, my mother didn't give me a lot of advice or words of what to do next, except for these couple of thoughts: It's going to be hard for a while, but trust God and stay focused on his love for you and the girls. She'd call on a regular basis to check on us and she left each conversation with the question, "Are you staying focused." I knew what she meant. Don't get caught up in your grieving so much that you can't see God or feel His presence. It was hard. Trying to raise two beautiful daughters as a single parent. I didn't do hair. Later, God sent to me another wonderful woman who became my wife with a fantastic daughter who became my bonus daughter, and we are all doing well. My mother was right.

The last year of mother's life was particularly difficult. My sister was the primary caregiver as I was living in New York. I helped as much as I could financially and in other ways. We talked just about every day even though she was in hospice. She was conscious most of her final days. Two months before her passing, she worked on presidential candidate Barak Obama's campaign. When I chided her for getting up out of bed to go work on his campaign, she said, " I had to do it. You gotta help the boy." As I said, she was tough. We'd talk about so many things during those final days and how she was looking forward to seeing Jesus, her savior. She told me that next to Mary she had the best son. I was with her most of her final days, but I missed her taking her last breath even though she had lapsed into unconsciousness the last couple of days. I had to return to New York for one day and then to return to Denver the next. While I was gone, literally overnight, my sister called to tell me that mother had transitioned. To this day, I profoundly regret not being there with her when she took her last breath. The irony is that I was with my father at his bedside when he took his. I preached her eulogy and referred to her as my "First Friend."

I don't remember my first suckling at my mother's breast, but I shall never forget our last goodbye.

Thank you, Mother.

With daughter
Janice & son Reggie

Portrait 1995

Portait

Mertis and Reggie

With Reggie and
Ceotis Tuggle 2005

Speaking at her
80th birthday party
in 2007

BETTYE JANE HILL

By: Tina Hodges

Queenin'

My mama, Bettye Jane (BJ), was born in 1929 to a man named King David Thames and a woman named Kate. B.J. was the oldest of four children – proud and fiercely protective of her family. It is through the family stories I grew up with and the personalities that surrounded and shaped my mother that I'm able to explain the essence of who I am today.

The Thames (or Tims- like the river) family were hardworking, God-fearing folks who had a voracious love for books and a desire to see their children get a good education. They lived in a military town, Fayetteville, NC. Grandma Kate was a housewife who cooked, cleaned, and sewed beautiful dresses for her girls and suits for her one and only son.

Granddad, King David, worked in a factory plant for 40 plus years. On Fridays he would give most, but not all, of his paycheck to Kate for the household. What he kept in his pocket, he drank up through the weekend. Monday mornings found him faithfully back at work. B.J. loved her daddy who swore she was his favorite, and she chose to remember only the good things about him. King David died a week before I was born and I always wished I'd had more of a chance to get to know him.

Here's how Mama described her young life: she was the most popular, the best dancer, and the best roller skater. She was the president of her class, a charter member of the Big Six (the club for cool kids), and smart as a whip. She was a proud graduate, first of E.E. Smith High School and then North Carolina A&T State University, the first among her siblings to finish college: all siblings would eventually get secondary degrees. She was a proud and active alumna of both schools – Aggie Pride! She enjoyed the camaraderie of these relationships and treasured friends and classmates for her entire life. Never accused of being shy, reserved, or modest, Mama embraced life with gusto!

My Favorite Stories

Mama had a terrible stuttering problem when she was young, and she was teased all the time. With hard work and the help of a favorite English teacher, E.J. Fowler, Mama was able to rid herself of the problem, except on the rare occasion when she became anxious. It never slowed her down however, and she always remained sensitive and helpful to fellow stutterers she met along the way.

A smart and savvy businesswoman who never wasted a dollar, Mama eventually became Chief of the Family Division for the Juvenile Court of the District of Columbia. She hired many professionals who had graduated from HBCUs just as she had. A few had police records from years of civil rights marches and protests, their eligibility for government jobs was in question. Mama quietly made sure they weren't penalized for their years of lawful civil disobedience. She both hired and promoted them. Many, now retired, have remained eternally grateful. My Mama was always proud of that.

Sadly, my parents' marriage dissolved and Mama found herself divorced with three kids under the age of 12. Surprisingly, she had never learned to drive. That didn't stop her though. She bought a car, had the dealer park it in front of the house, and then spent the next three months learning to drive. She never learned to parallel park however, and after two failed attempts, the instructor simply gave up and granted her a license! I remember the first time she drove us to McDonalds;

it was an awesome day! And each evening when Mama came home from work the teenage boys in the neighborhood waited excitedly for her to pull up so they could direct her into her parking spot out front. In fact, helping my Mama park became a daily neighborhood event! She always laughed at the teasing, head held high.

Mama always waited until one or two days before Christmas to buy a tree because they were cheaper by then. But they were also picked over and frankly, pretty sad to look at. Many a year, friends would make sure to come by to laugh at our annual Charlie Brown Christmas tree. But Mama would always point to the many gifts under that tree and assure them that our family would have the last laugh.

Mama had at least eight total hip replacements in her life; so many, in fact, that I honestly began to lose track. All included long, slow, painful rehabs and weeks of recovery; back then hip surgeries were rarely performed and the materials weren't especially durable. For years Mama needed a cane on the days her hip bothered her most. But that, and other life challenges never stopped my Mama from wearing her chic ensembles, matching outfits and jewelry. And the constant pain never ruined her joy or love for life and laughter.

So when I look in the mirror, I see her reflection, not so much physically but rather her spirit and zest for life. Her determination not to stay down when knocked down, to care about and for others, to judge a person on their character rather than their possessions, and to believe in the power of God to know and heal all things.

It is because of her greatness that I, and my own children, continue to shine, and we all know it! Cheers to you, Mama.

Bettye Jane (BJ) Hill

(1929-2009)

WILHELMINA "BILLIE" RICHARDSON BRODIE

By: Michelle Brodie Vereen

This was the woman I watched. And what did I see, hear, and infuse into my corporal being of mind, body, and soul that made me who I am and whom I aspire to be? A whole heck of a lot. Because a life does not start in a vacuum, let's go back a little way.

My mother was the first of two daughters born in 1936 in Augusta, GA to Canute Mena Richardson and Josephine Allen Richardson. I've never met another Canute in my entire life, probably for a reason. He was an immigrant to this country from Blue Fields, Nicaragua. He came at the age of fourteen to stay and study with a cousin who'd already been accepted to college. Long story short, that didn't work out and he ended up having to go to work and to put himself through school. He graduated from Morris Brown University and went on to receive a Master of Arts from Columbia University in 1945. What I remember about him is that he was very soft-spoken and although he spoke English, my young mind did not understand why his words didn't sound like our words. I grew to understand that English was not his native tongue so he still spoke with a Spanish accent.

My grandmother, Josephine Allen Richardson, was born in Augusta in 1907. Education was paramount in her family, so she graduated from Haines Institute, later Lucy Laney High School, in Augusta and went on to Atlanta University. As there were not many professional opportunities for black women at that time, she became a teacher.

Later she became the Registrar for Paine College and Canute became the Vice-President.

Let's start with that name of hers. Whew. It's a mouthful. Wilhelmina, after her maternal grandfather William. Wimberly, after her maternal great grandfather, Joe Wimberly, the Caucasian carpetbagger from Ohio who came to the South to assist in Reconstruction. Joe Wimberly met my great-great grandmother and started a family, in the South.

With that backdrop, the expectation for the Richardson girls to excel in education was enormous. My mother's sister, Lois Adele, was born two years after my mother. At the age of ten, my aunt Lois died. My grandmother would tell of the day that she sent the girls off to school, like any normal day, and one never came home. Lois was on the playground and suffered a fatal aneurysm. This loss forever altered the lives of this family. It sent my grandmother into premature menopause at the age of thirty-something. She never had another menstrual cycle after that day. My grandfather was the stoic Spanish man, so he never really spoke about my aunt to me. The expectation to excel in school and in life was solely and squarely heaped onto my mother's shoulders.

My mother and I would later speak about how, at the age of 12, she was not prepared for that burden. There were only two years between them, she'd lost her sister, her best friend, and her confidant. Therefore, she rebelled. As I was older, and had my own children, my grandmother would tell my sister and me of the "difficulties" she and my grandfather had with my mother. Those "difficulties" they dealt with in the fifties are now part and parcel to raising teenagers today. Those "difficulties" included things like underage drinking, smoking (cigarettes, no less), missing curfew, and hanging out with a general wild child, so to speak. So as not to sully the reputation of the family, off to boarding school went my mother! She graduated from Mather Academy in Sumter, SC and met life-long friends who are still my "aunties" to this date. Mom then graduated from Howard University and went on to get her Master of Science in Library Education from The Atlanta University.

My mother has been deceased for three years. In preparing to write this remembrance on the woman I watched, I pulled out her funeral program for the first time since the funeral. It is appropriately titled "A Service of Thanksgiving For a Life's Task Faithfully Discharged." My mother wrote her own obituary and entitled it "Life is a Journey." Reading entire seventy-something years of a life encapsulated in two-hundred and fifteen words makes me wonder what two-hundred words will define the life she gave to me. Of course those two-hundred and fifteen words cannot do justice to ALL of the education, the accomplishments, the memberships in various organizations, the offspring and their offspring, the stumbles, the falls, the disappointments, the struggle, the service, and eventually the climb to the summit.

The Woman I Watched introduced me to reading at a very early age. (Duuhhh. She was a librarian). In those times that I find myself fumbling and stumbling about due to life's vagaries and vicissitudes, I inevitably return to that one book that makes all things right with the world. The one book I can always count on to get me back on track and on my way. For most, it's the Bible. Now, don't get me wrong, it's got some good stuff in there too. Now, Mom wasn't big on church but we went. But if you need a real pick me up, go get Dr. Seuss's "Oh, The Places You Will Go." Mom and I shared the same love of suspense, crime, detective, legal, and medical thrillers. I eventually branched out into some non-fiction and poetry as well.

My experience of my watching my mother and her legacy on my life is immeasurable in every way imaginable. I've always felt a connection to the Langston Hughes Poem "Mother to Son" because, "Life for me ain't been no crystal stair." This life bestowed upon me has for certain had its "fair share of tacks, and splinters, and boards torn up."

My parents were both educated professionals. I get my math and science skills from my father (and that's a whole 'nother story). But from my mother, I get everything else. When I examine her unwavering expectation in my ability to excel, I am profoundly grateful. As a little black girl who aspired to be an engineer in the early 1980s, who chose a university that was not an HBCU, I wonder if I'd let my daughter make the same decision. My parents were products of the Civil Rights Movement, having attended Atlanta University at the height of Dr. Martin Luther King's involvement. When I told my parents I wanted to be a chemical engineer, they said "Fine." When I told them I'd applied to Georgia Tech, they said "Fine." When I told them I'd applied to Boston University, they said "Fine." When I told them I'd applied to Clemson University, they said "Fine." Now that I think about it, neither one of them helped me, guided me, or offered any advice. Seems like now, we're doing it all for our kids. Neither one of them, both of whom had graduated from HBCUs, ever discouraged nor encouraged me to attend a HBCU, where undoubtedly I would have had more educational support and a totally different experience. However, I do know that what they marched for, fought for, and were arrested for, was the opportunity I had been afforded – to go to ANY school that I wanted. For that I am grateful that they supported my decision to attend Clemson University. I met the most wonderful friend there who later became my roommate. She was on her own journey so our time together in that circumstance was brief, but we remain lifelong friends, (Wink. Wink). Oh, and I did change my major to Ceramic Engineering ('cause life for me was no crystal stairs). I graduated. Period. Thanks, Mom.

After about ten years of working in the engineering field, the family bug of teaching and service bit me. We were still reading legal thrillers so I decided that I wanted to go to law school. What was I thinking? I was thinking that I could do anything, even though I had a full-time job, a kid in kindergarten, a sometimes (and sometimes not) helpful husband. I'm thinking this would have been a good time for her to speak up. Some days I'd call my mother because I was so overwhelmed with work, the kids, their activities, and school. She would always remind me that it was only temporary and that I wasn't given any more than I could handle. And if I couldn't handle it, to put it down. I truly attribute my graduation from law school to the early introduction to reading. Since I had been reading for so long, I could read fast. Thanks, Mom.

Although my Mom wasn't big on attending church, she was big on being of service to those around her. After a long battle with alcoholism, my mother became a sponsor of other men and women battling the disease of addiction. As she was the Media Specialist at the high school I attended, my mother knew the boys in the school and since they were the boys in our neighborhood, she also knew the predicaments they were having. After I went off to college, she started a club for the black males in the school. It was called "The Change Club." I would come home on school breaks and there would be 10 or 15 young men in my mother's living room. I wonder why she didn't start that club until after I'd left for college. Hmmm. One of those members of that club, Keith Hammond, wrote of my mother in his book "Built to Be Broken." I think it was the first time that I could understand her impact on young people. Thanks, Mom.

So now here we are, trying to have the same impact on the lives of young people. My sister, Lisa Norwood, is the Assistant Principal, after having been a teacher for many years at the same high school we attended. It is the same high school that retired my mother. My legal career has been spent primarily in the public sector. For the past twenty years, I've represented children; children accused of delinquent acts; children who've been abused or neglected; and children whose parents are in raging custody wars. We try every day to touch a young person's life in such a way that they are positively impacted by our contact. Thanks, Mom.

The Woman I Watched showed me how to succeed, how to fall, how to fail, how to bend without breaking, and how to be of service in this thing called life. If it hadn't already been written, she would have most certainly said, "You have brains in your head. You have feet in your shoes. You can steer yourself any direction you choose. You're on your own. And you know what you know. And YOU are the one who'll decide where to go..." I am still working on my two-hundred and fifteen words. Thanks, Mom.

Wilhelmina "Billie" Brodie
(1936-2015)

With Mother, Grandmother, and Michelle
circa 1964

DIANE ROBINSON NEAL

By: Elonda Neal & Tara Edwards

As Mother

Diane C. Neal grew up in the Midwest in Sioux City, Iowa born to Allen and Mable Robinson on February 25, 1945. She has one older brother named Allen Robinson, Jr. She grew up Catholic, attended Catholic schools, and converted to Baptist during her adulthood. She is the mother of three children: Duane (Junior), Derrick, and Elonda; and the proud grandmother of two grandchildren and two great-grandchildren. She is happily married to Roosevelt Neal, Jr., and is a proud member of Salem Bible Church, Atlanta, GA where she is a Deacon. She is woman of God, who has strong morals and character.

Wanting a better life for herself and family, she was faced with a tough decision regarding moving from Iowa to Chicago. This decision was extremely difficult for mom because it meant moving away from home for the first time and leaving her comfort zone. As difficult as the decision was she choose to relocate to Chicago and after she settled into her new community she decided that she wanted to work with children. Mom was hired as a teacher's assistant at Wicker Park Elementary School in Chicago. My brother and I also attended the same school. While working as a teacher's assistant she had the vision of someday owning her own childcare center.

A couple of years later my dad was offered a job in Atlanta, and my mom believed that moving to Atlanta would be a great opportunity for our entire family.

In the summer of 1979 my family moved to Atlanta, GA, where we all still reside. After getting settled in Atlanta mom took a job in retail for a few years. I laugh every time I hear her say, that she knew retail was not her calling, and that she knew that retail was not her calling. After regrouping and getting her thoughts and dreams back on track she realized she still desired to work with children, so she convinced my Dad to allow her to start an in-home daycare business in the small apartment they lived in. She didn't know how she would get it started or how she would convince parents that she was trustworthy and would take good care of their children. She networked while working retail and met two mothers who were looking for someone to watch children. Each mother at that time had one child.

After having a few meetings with the mothers, Mom launched her in-home daycare. Finally! She was living her dream of owning her own business, being her own boss, and working with children. Within one year she had grown from taking care of two children to four. All marketing for moms' daycare business was by word of mouth, and all daycare slots were filled by referrals from the current parents.

Becoming homeowners in the affluent East Cobb community in Marietta, GA, just 17 miles northwest of the city of Atlanta was a big accomplishment for my parents. This move ensured that my brother and I would attend some of the finest schools in the state and in some cases the county, and this move also allowed my mom to expand her in-home daycare business. She was able to convert our basement into the daycare, making it a safe haven for children. Diane's Daycare grew from four children to eight children, and there was always a waiting list. She earned the trust and respect of the parents whose children she watched and nurtured and she honored her commitment. Mom was a tremendous support system to "her parents", as she referred to them.   She was genuinely concerned about the wellbeing of the children she kept, and also about the families of those children. She allowed parents to arrive as early as 6 am if needed, and for some parents who were attending school, she allowed pick up after 8 pm. No matter what time they arrived, she would always have a smile on her face and joy in her heart, and she would have bathed and fed the children so that when the parents got home all they had to do was put the child to bed. She was amazing!

The children felt my mother's love, and most of them responded to her as if she was their second mother. While watching and assisting her with running her daycare, I was able to witness another side of love that my mother provided. That was love of family. I learned from the woman I watched the importance of loving and always supporting family.

I often heard mom say, "A family that prays together stays together."

Diane's Daycare was in business for over 30 years when she decided to retire to spend more time with our family; and in particular my grand nieces. During those 30 years Mom extended our family by taking great care of those children. Diane's Daycare graduated an awesome group of children who remain friends to this day; some having met at the precious age of six weeks old.

Mom has attended high school and college graduations, and weddings of the children she cared for. 100% of the children from Diane's Day Care graduated from high school and college. Many of them attended graduate school and graduated with Masters Degrees. Some are now parents themselves and have brought their children to meet Mrs. Diane and my dad, Mr. Neal. To this day, her daycare children keep in touch with her by calling, sending cards, and even stopping by to get a hug from her; they say she gives the best hugs!

During a family tragedy Mom demonstrated how family should unite when a loved one is taken away unexpectedly. I remember saying to myself, "How is mom holding up after losing her child?" She was a pillar of strength; never showing any signs of weakness; only strength and composure. I also remember the smile on her face after seeing the parents of her daycare children showing up for the funeral and couldn't believe all the love she received during that time. I never knew how many different hats a mother could wear, until I saw her sit on a witness stand and talk about her deceased son. It took a great deal of faith in God; and her faith was tested. Watching her go through that tragedy made me want to have the strength I saw exhibited by her.

Later in her years she had to make another big decision in having two full knee replacements. She'd never had any type of major surgery before in her entire life. She made the decision to have both knees replaced within three months apart. It was such a joyous occasion after mom made her decision. We knew this procedure would enable our very strong and resilient mother to make an amazing comeback.

It was absolutely amazing and such a joy to see Mom bounce back after the first knee replacement. It was amazing to see her fight back and push through intense physical therapy. She did not give up and she worked hard every day. During this process she relied on her dependency on God to guide and to protect her.

Diane Neal has inspired me by showing that it doesn't matter where you come from, or what you do or don't have; it's all about making the best out of what you have, and building your empire on that foundation.

She loves her life so dearly, and everyone with whom she shares it. Her love and respect for my father is incredibly strong. She is absolutely the strongest person I know, and I hope to exhibit that same strength some day. Diane's career was not just a means to a paycheck, but something she loved and was truly passionate about. Diane surrounded herself with family and friends who she considered to be family. That is not to say that she is never upset or sad. Mom never seems to let it get in the way of her overall happiness.

She instilled in me such self-confidence and self-worth, and she made me believe that I could do anything I wanted to do, and when I faltered, she was always there to hold my hand. I'll never forget the time when I wanted to apply for graduate school and was scared to apply and step out on faith. She told me that I could do it, and that God had my back, He would see me through the program, and I would not be a failure. If I just took one class at a time, she would still love and support me the same. Those words of encouragement allowed me to put one foot in front of the other and pound the pavement, following my dream. I always knew that she would always be proud of me no matter what, and that allowed me to find my way and happiness.

Mom always spoke up when something is wrong and she always made sure that it got straightened out. She would guide me on how to approach my friends when I was mad, sad, or feeling bad. I would come away from it learning a major life lesson. I know at times I do that less as an adult, and I'm trying to change that because I know how much happier and healthier I can be as a result of it. No matter how much I'm hurt at the time, I want to always be able to stand up for myself and for those whom I love.

She also inspired me because she always lives by her beliefs and values. Her number one priority is her relationship with GOD and then her family, which has been instilled in me as well. What I have learned is the fact that you would jump in front of a moving bullet if it meant that it spared your husband and/or your children. By living by her values, Diane has done more than say, "Family comes first," she has lived it. This has most definitely taught me to be true to myself, to honor my values to live my passion, to wait for the right man to come along; one that deserves to be with my wonderfully loving and silly family and me, and to choose to surround myself with those that possess peace, positivity, and happiness. I don't and will not waiver on any of those morals, because Diane has been my role model my entire life.

As Grandmother

I've contemplated many ways to begin this chapter of my life and as painful and hesitant as I am to share this part of my family, I am going to. Don't get me wrong, my story is not all bad or unhappy; it is a story of a journey with a woman who is at the least incredible. However, nothing good ever comes from anything easy or without a struggle and with struggle comes pain and finding power within ourselves. This is the first time I have ever spoken publicly of this event, therefore, most of what I say will be difficult, but it is a major part of why that I am sharing The woman from my village, the woman I watched my Grandmother Diane; mother to my father, great-grandmother to my children, and matriarch of the Neal women!

First Memory: The Funeral

As my sister, Tiana and I sat with our mother in the front pew of a small church in Savannah, Georgia on the base at Hunter Army Airfield, I saw familiar and unfamiliar faces, people I hadn't seen in a very long time, people that typically (in my nine-year-old mind) shouldn't be in the same setting with each other. I have on a borrowed dress from my best friend at the time. I barely know what's going on; I'm just taking it all in. As the church fills with solemn faces and tears, I see beautiful flowers and I notice a pink and white ribbon with a bow that says "Daddy" inside the casket. In that moment (it still amazes me) all I could think was, "I don't remember picking that out." See, even at nine, I noticed everything and focused on anything that would distract me from how I really felt. I had this innate ability to put "me" aside and portray the "strong" mentality. While everyone else was crying and sad, I couldn't cry. I remember I kept asking myself, "Why can't I cry?" Then it happened, at that moment the whole church was filled with emotion when my Grandma Diane walked through the door with my grandfather (better known as Gramps) holding her up.

My grandmother let out the shrillest most heartbreaking scream; it made the whole room feel all the sadness, grief, agony, anger, disbelief, regret, despair, and most of all LOVE that she had for the young man lying in the coffin. It has been twenty five years and I will never forget that moment. I was facing the back of the church looking at her and at that moment the enormity of the circumstance hit me like a ton of bricks and it slapped me into reality like the crack of a whip. My grandmother had to bury her son; her 29-year-old son who didn't just die from illness or an accident, he was murdered; taken without notice, altering our lives forever. I no longer had to ask myself why I couldn't cry because it all made sense to me in that moment and even if I never cried for me, I would always cry for her pain. Suddenly, the events from the days leading up to the funeral flashed before me—being awakened in the middle of the night by MP's knocking on our door to deliver the news of my father's death; my grandmother experiencing the same visit—hearing from my Aunt Elonda that he was shot multiple times; my grandmother had to listen to the same information—the limousine ride to the funeral that I was excited to experience, my aunt whispering to me, "There are better ways to ride in a limousine;" my grandmother had to experience that same ride. This unbearable pain, masked by blind innocence, and the love and protection of my grandmother. I was so well protected during this time I couldn't even see how sad she was until that moment. She unknowingly taught me at that time that being completely broken, at rock bottom, and being "weak" was perfectly fine and that the mentality of what I was viewing as "strong" was merely a metaphor for people who hide their emotions. As I heard a family member say later that day, "Parents aren't supposed to outlive their kids." So now a fact that I must live with is that I have joined the rest of my family and especially my Grandmother Diane in knowing and continuing to live with the fact that I have outlived my father. These events resonated with me and gave me a perspective of life that many people never have to encounter. The rest of that church service is a complete blur and we haven't ever talked about that day with each other, but my grandmother unknowingly taught me a great lesson that day, a lesson that has and will shape me for the rest of my days.

That day was a pivotal day for me for more reasons than it being my father's funeral and burial. This is the most remembered event in my life. I have replayed that day over and over throughout the years. Mainly so I won't forget, but also because it was the first time I saw most of my family members cry, the main one being my grandmother. Strength comes in all shapes and forms and everyone has their own challenges to build strength from. I always say that we are all dealt a hand of cards in life and it's up to us on how we play our hand that determines our journey. My grandmother was dealt a hand that unfortunately involved her losing a child. Watching her strength and willpower to overcome those emotions and move forward with life unwittingly gave me strength to keep on without a father. I felt it in the way she would hold me tight and kiss my forehead. I felt it in every trip that she planned for us and how she nurtured us on every summer and winter vacation at her house. I felt her devotion and determination to not let any of the events in life affect us; that we would always know that we were loved and cared for with or without our father.

Second Memory: Living Situation

Not long after my father passed away, my mom, sister, and I moved to Marietta, GA to be closer to my grandparents. My mom lasted six months in the city before she was ready to move back to Savannah. I was in second grade and it was decided that I would continue the school year in Marietta and live with my grandparents. It was during this time that I experienced a different side of my grandmother that I had never seen before. (I seem to be able to pull this side out in a lot of people close to me, but that's another story for another day.) This memory is when my grandmother had to be strict with me and it ended up with me having one of my most epic meltdowns. I don't recall what started the disciplinary action, but I can assume I wasn't getting my way with something. I remember my grandmother not budging on her decision and me getting more and more upset. I ended up crying hysterically and was made to stay in my room for the night. I couldn't believe the one who always spoiled me and gave me anything I wanted or needed was being completely unapproachable. I cried so hard, I fell asleep in the middle of the day and slept all night. I don't recall having an argument that massive with her ever again, but I do remember that I knew well enough not to ever try that with her again.

Everyone has their own opinion on what a strong woman is and how they gauge their ability to be strong. In my opinion, a strong woman can be stern and hold her ground. A strong woman knows what battles are best to choose. A strong woman doesn't have to say much or yell to get her point across. A strong woman can command respect with one look. I saw a different side to my grandmother that day. Always nurturing, always consistent, and undeniably strong..

Nurturer

As we all know, everyone measures success differently. A good friend once told me that being content in life does not mean you are settling, it means that you are one with God and when you fully trust in the Lord then what you have will always be enough. This is how I would describe my grandmother's life and this is something that I am still striving for today. Until about two years ago, my grandmother ran an in-home daycare for as long as I could remember. Every child that came through that house was like a sister or brother to my sister and I. They were a part of our family. That is how my grandmother operates; if you know her, then you are family. I remember spending summer vacations with her and my Gramps and helping prepare lunches for the toddlers and feeding the infants. She taught me how to nurture them and together we made them feel like they were home while their parents were away. We built long lasting relationships with all of the children that "Mrs. Diane" had a hand in rearing. I am still friends with several of those children to this day and we all keep up with each other. All of the families still pop up and visit my grandmother whenever they are in the area. This makes me the most proud of my grandmother. This is the type of person that I strive to be in my life; I want to touch people's lives so much that they will visit me just because and call me just to check on me. That shows how influential of a person she is and was to them during a portion their lives. It is truly admirable and I love reminiscing with my extended siblings about funny moments with her and hearing certain memories that they have of her that align with my feelings as her grandchild.

In my later years, I choose to only see the good in people and what their intentions are. This is largely due to what I observed in my grandmother. When I think of my grandma I think of how much I love her laugh. It is loud and boisterous, much like the sound of my own laughter. It reminds me of where I come from and that I belong to a long line of women who love to be happy and don't mind being the loudest one in the room. In addition to her laughter, I love how passionate she is about her family. Her passion intensifies if she sees that one of her children or grandchildren are wronged and treated unjustly. That is when the feisty and fierce part of her comes out. She does not have a problem with letting you know how she feels in those moments and to hear her yell at her great-granddaughter's soccer games is a comedy show all by itself. It warms my heart to think of all the passion she has. She genuinely wants her family to be happy and stress free. She is constantly telling me, "Now, Baby, you take care of yourself now you hear me? I mean it!" She is constantly emphasizing that to me. Another gesture of love that I love about my Grandma is how she will call a couple times during the week just to leave you a voicemail message, and if you answer the call it completely throws her off. She just wants to leave a message without "bothering" you just so you know she is thinking of you. Grandma Diane is always consistent and I always know that for every holiday and birthday we usually get at least two cards and a check with a "lunch on us" message every year. It never fails and makes me smile every time. I love the way that she will insert our names on the card and double underline certain words or phrases written on the card just so you know that the card was intentionally and purposely chosen for you. It is a compilation of all of the small things that add up to make you feel special and the sheer simplicity is the best part of it. She's consistent and always there when you don't even know you need her. For as long as I can remember my grandmother has always been there for us. A rock that is always consistent. Anything you ask of her, she will do it to the best of her ability. I sometimes find myself purposely not mentioning things to her just so she won't volunteer or try to go out of her way to make it happen for us.

Protector

The best attribute that I acquired from my grandmother is being a protector of the people I love. There are many trials, life issues, and general dilemmas that my grandmother protected me from while I was growing up. Knowing what I know now, I appreciate that about her; protecting us from the cold truths of the world and the burdens that can bring on a person. She carried all of those burdens for her children and grandchildren. I truly believe that is why I always tend to look at the good side of people and not let the negative side get to me as much. I cannot remember a time when I ever heard her focus on the negative about anyone. I'm not saying she hasn't had her moments, but I haven't witnessed this myself. Sometimes I feel like I was shielded too much, but I see now that as a protector for my children, I understand why. Therefore, I would like to say thank you to my grandmother for being a stoic rock that was always there to protect me when I didn't know I needed protecting.

My grandmother also protected all of her extended children that she babysat as well as their parents. I remember her always being there for them before and after hours providing her care and love, as it was needed. Everyone who knows her can go to her for advice and know that they will get the honest answers to help solve their problems, whether you want to hear it or not. The advice she gave was always out of love.

Facing Fears

I have learned and I am still learning that if we don't face our fears we will stay the same; and that being scared means you are about to do something that is brave and will make you a better person. I don't remember a time that I saw my grandmother walk on her own or without a struggle from the pain in her knees. I never had the guts to ask her why it was difficult for her to walk or bend her knees, it was just one of those things that we accepted and thought there wasn't an option for her. I never realized until I was older that she suffered constant pain in her knees caused by arthritis. It wasn't until my uncle started pushing for her to get some help that they found out that she basically needed a double knee replacement and quickly! She was so afraid of what they may say and what the surgery involved that she avoided it for years. She sat in constant pain year in and year out, because of her own fears; fear of the unknown. I didn't need proof that my grandmother was strong and could withstand the toughest of situations, but knowing that all of her pain was unnecessary blew my mind. The phrase that comes to mind is, "One tough cookie!" I am proud to say that with support and a little pushing from her children, my grandmother successfully went through not one, but two knee replacement surgeries within several months of each other. She not only faced her fears and went through the surgeries and the grueling physical therapy that came along with them, the surgeon commented that her knees were the worst he had seen in his tenure as a surgeon and that he couldn't believe she went that long in pain with how they looked. My grandmother now walks on her own and can even walk up and down stairs. She turned her fears into something better for herself and it is great to see her improving each day with her stamina and strength. I pray that she continues to find strength in her actions and carries those feelings with her in future decisions that need to be made for her to be the best her that she can be.

Partner in Crime

I find it hard to speak of my grandmother without mentioning my Gramps as well. They come as a package deal in my mind and they have been each other's rock for ages. They often make a joke about how everyone referred to my sister and I, and subsequently my two daughters, Trinity and Trew, as "The Girls," and how it always sounds like they are talking about a singing group. This is how I feel when I speak of "Gramps and Grandma;" it sounds like a band to me. I always refer to them in this way because they are one. Gramps always takes care of her and he is just as much of a nurturer as she is. Having faith in God and putting Him at the center of their relationship is what has kept them together for so long. Once again, that's another great lesson that my grandmother has taught me. They are true partners and will do whatever is necessary to keep the family together. They create a huge sense of togetherness that is comforting and soothing to be around. They are a perfect example of true love and what it means to commit to each other for eternity. Together they have raised a great family and have provided a solid foundation for my girls.. Their house is my home base and I always feel like I've arrived "home" when I visit. They have given me the best memories, the best vacations, the best birthdays, the best holidays, and the best "just because" moments. They are the embodiment of synergy and their family-centered traditions make us all who we are. I don't know what my grandmother considers her greatest achievement in life, but I believe it should be maintaining the commitment of marriage and proving that longevity in relationships provide the best rewards that we can ask for. Experiences that we have in life are what make us who we are and afford us the ability to give advice and give us the opportunity to set an example for generations to come.

I don't know everything about my grandmother's life; my memories of her begin at age nine. However, I feel like the parts of her that I do know are enough and explain why I am they way I am today. My grandmother is the ultimate nurturer, the rock of our family whether she knows it or not. She is our glue and without her there are so many experiences and occasions that would not have been possible. When I look back at her life, I know that it has had its ups and downs. In my opinion, it is because of all of those emotions and experiences that she is the matriarch that she is today for all of us that have been touched by her. The levels of obstacles that she has had to overcome and how she overcame them fill me with faith and hope each day. I have learned from her that no matter what we go through, there is always someone else out there who has it worse than we do. We have each other and no matter what, we all can fall back on her when we need to. The stability that she has provided is never ending and I always know that she will be there for all of us. We don't get to choose our family. God knows exactly what our paths will be and why we are placed with certain people. All I can say is, I wouldn't change my family or our struggles for anything in the world. We are unique, dynamic, and fierce because that is what we have been taught. Approach every fear head on and quietly let our past guide us into who we want to be in the future.

Diane, Roosevelt & Elonda

With Tara, Roosevelt, & Elonda

Diane, Roosevelt & Tiana

With Elonda

CATHERINE P. ROBINSON

By: Cynthia Robinson Alexander

Extremely complex is the best way to describe my relationship with my mom. For anyone to truly understand our mother-daughter relationship, you must know a little about Mom's life and my immediate family.

I was the fourth of five children, the only daughter of the family. Mom's formal schooling stopped when she graduated from the eighth grade. Mom's mother died when she was 12-years-old, and her father remarried and moved mom and her two older sisters from South Georgia to South Jersey. Mom's stepmother had family members who were farmers in South Georgia who went north to find a better life and better jobs. Mom and her stepmother's relationship was cordial at best.

By the time Mom was eighteen she had three babies and was married to someone who rarely worked. Life was extremely hard; they had no money. It was through the grace of God, the goodwill of her family, and personal grit and determination that Mom was able to provide the bare minimum of food and shelter for her sons and herself.

After years of tirelessly working and mothering her three sons by herself, Mom divorced her first husband and met and married my father. My younger brother (who is two years younger than me) and I are the product of their union. There is a ten-year gap between the youngest of my three older brothers and me, and fifteen years difference between my oldest brother and me. Despite this wide spread in ages and having different fathers, my parents lovingly raised all of us as one family.

One Halloween night, my birth made my parents and three older brothers extremely happy. I am always reminded they all prayed for a daughter and a sister; and I arrived. Soon after my birth, one of my brothers took a picture of me to class for show and tell; he was thrilled to have a sister. Both of my parents doted on me and were extremely proud to have a daughter. In many ways, my family treated me as one of the favorites; the "favorite" and only daughter and sister, the "favorite" niece, cousin, and granddaughter.

All of this affection and doting brought big expectations for me from my family and especially my Mom. From an early age, I realized that my mother lived her life through me. My possessions, my travels, and accomplishments – all became hers as well. My mom always expressed her plans for me, to go to college and to become someone. Growing up in a rural farming community in South Jersey, I shared my Mom's dreams of going away. I accepted that college was the way out. Coupled that with the fact that, as with many teenagers, I thought I knew much more than my eighth grade-educated mom, and needed to forge ahead with my life. I was always on a mission, scheming to leave as soon as I graduated high school.

Mom used to say to me that all she expected of me was to be a mother. I guess that was her backhand way of using reverse psychology so that I would not become a teenage mother like her. All I can say is that it made me mad as ever and drove me to be even more deliberate in my escape from my parent's house, my mom in particular. With that said, I was always very compliant and rarely got into any type of serious trouble. The tension in the house was that my mom and I were two VERY strong willed women. My entire family understood and would jokingly observe the tension and the tumultuous verbal exchanges that occurred between mom and me. Of course, I was always right, and Mom was always wrong. My irritation with my mom ranged from how she spoke, including the fact that she did not pronounce certain words correctly, her lack of style in not wearing the latest clothing fads, and her lack of sophistication about worldly events.

We were not an outwardly hugging and loving mother and daughter. For the most part, I was always respectful, but it was dutiful respect with an attitude. I did everything I could that would assure my escape from my rural South Jersey upbringing, and my mom in particular. I was labeled and classified as gifted early in school therefore, I worked on getting the best grades possible. I joined as many clubs as possible because that meant I could spend more time away from our home, hanging out with my various club members. I was not athletic, being only 5 feet, 4 inches and weighing less than 90 pounds. I was not graceful, and lacked musical or dancing talents. My family and friends referred to me as being cute, but not beautiful, something in hindsight I am most thankful for because I am sure my mom would have insisted on me entering countless beauty contests.

Upon graduating from high school with honors and serving as one of the featured speakers for the occasion, I immediately left my home. I spent the summer after graduation in a transitional educational program at Brown University. I told my mom it was to help me transition to being in college, but the real reason I wanted to participate was to get away from her and my environment. Other than coming home for one or two summers when I absolutely had no other place to go, I never returned home. The longest period I spent back home with my parents was when I returned home six months prior to getting married. My stays were always limited to no more than three days to assure peace between my mom and me. Beyond that third day, we were destined to engage in a disagreement over something. It could be the way I cut my hair, the fact that I added a second hole to my earlobes - anything. My father would always stay neutral during these episodes and say, "You know how your mother is."

After getting married, I had absolutely no reservations in moving to Atlanta, Georgia. My thoughts were to get far enough away from my mom not to have to deal with her on a daily basis but close enough that we could drive and visit at least once or twice a year. My mom was not happy about our decision to relocate from Boston to Atlanta. She told my husband, "How dare you take my only daughter to that forsaken place? You don't have to worry about me knocking on your back door, I do not intend to ever return to Georgia. Why didn't you and my daughter consider going to Texas or California?" At that time, I never envisioned the events that would unfold in our lives.

After about twenty years of being married and having two sons of my own, my father died unexpectedly and Mom moved south to spend her last ten years living with my family and me, in her words, "in god-forsaken Atlanta." At first Mom would come to Atlanta for holidays and vacations. Ultimately, Mom's visits extended into full relocation.

What a blessing it was, in hindsight, for me to spend those last ten years with my mom. Do not get confused, some days it was pure hell, to say it mildly. God knew we needed each other and more importantly, God knew I needed my mom, more than she needed me. During those ten years, my mom became a part of my family in Atlanta and prepared me for life without her. Time spent with her showed me what a phenomenal women she really was and how fortunate for me that God connected us together for life and thereafter.

I always knew it, but I came to appreciate the sheer grit that my mom had, and that she was indeed a hard working wife and mother. She was the epitome of a working mother. She passed this trait on to all of her children, my four brothers and me. We understand that we were born on this earth to work hard for our families. Mom worked in a factory for over 35 years, making boxes and many times working double shifts (16 hours) at the glass factory and then she would come home and work in the family fields making sure the corn, beans, okra, tomatoes, and other vegetables growing on our family land were cultivated. To this day, my two remaining brothers and I are early risers; we cannot sleep past seven o'clock in the morning.

Mom always showered everyone she encountered with love and attention. Mom was straight talking and candid with everyone, especially those she loved. The harder the sting, the deeper the love she had for you. While I try my best to moderate the sting and to be diplomatic, everyone who meets me will say I speak my mind. Mom imparted great wisdom to those she met, young and old, and encouraged each person to be the very best they could be and to do the right thing always. Mom loved entertaining folk and celebrating life. And like Mom, I truly enjoy planning special events and entertaining at my home. Mom had an infectious laugh, dazzling smile, sharp wit even at 90 years of age. When she walked into a room, she would bring the house down with a quick comment that caused all activity in the room to cease. You would call it presence. I am still trying to master these traits. At sixty plus years, I am prayerful that like my mom I will live to be ninety. I pray I have a few more decades to master those unique character traits that my mom possessed.

Unequivocally, Mom's top priorities in life were the Lord and loving her family. She loved the Lord, and the Lord knew and loved her. She loved family and being with them; she shared generously. There are so many things that my mom taught me and that she shared with all that she met. I must admit, I am the person I am today because of my mom. Her determination that I become somebody, her insistence that I go as far as I can at whatever I try and if I fail; to go and try again.

All of my personal and professional accomplishments thus far in life are a direct result of the foundation Mom provided me from birth. I am a graduate of Brown, Harvard, and Boston Universities where I obtained an undergraduate, master, and law degrees, respectively. I have traveled the world, both professionally and personally. I have held senior level positions leading domestic and international owners and investors of commercial real estate. I am a mother, wife, sister, daughter, cousin, and friend. My primary goal for so long in life was not to be like my mom. With each passing year, I am astonished to look in the mirror, and see that I am more and more like her. What irony!

Food, Sustenance for the Soul

At a very early age, I came to understand from my mom that food not only provided nutrition for the body but also provided sustenance for the soul. In my family home, food served as the glue that held our family together. Food provided the nurturing that was the key to us surviving and thriving in life. For my family members and me, the connection between food and love is unwavering!

No one ever entered our home and left without eating something or leaving with a bag, basket, or crate of fresh vegetables or whatever was growing in the garden (all 30 acres), or found in the barn, refrigerator, or food cabinet. Whoever was present at dinnertime ate with us and ate as much as they liked. My memories are full of much laughter, discussion, heated political debates, and love centered on mealtime and food. Our family, our neighbors, and our friends were never hungry. Our bodies were filled with food and minds, spirits, and souls were filled with love.

As a teenager, I often wanted something other than what was prepared for the meal. I did not appreciate that there was always food available nor did I understand our blessings. But my mom taught me the value of feeding people and the goodwill it generates. What is so amazing, in hindsight, is that between my mom and dad, my dad was the better cook. However, Mom was the person most passionate about sharing food. No matter how little food was prepared or leftover, there was always plenty to share with whoever was present.

Food prepared in our home was wonderfully delicious! I hated Sunday dinner because it was always some form of roast beef. Roast Beef! Fast forward forty or more years, I crave to have one of those

Sunday dinners that always had two or three fresh vegetables, rice, and some form of potatoes and a huge roast. Did I mention there was always a pan of cornbread? And not the kind that came from a Jiffy box.

Mastering her senses of sight, smell, and taste, mom created those wonderful meals. These recipes were stored in her memory and nothing was ever written down. More importantly, mom was one of those women who never measured anything. The common direction she provided me, or anyone she was directing in her kitchen, was to add in the ingredients until it looked right. And what a wonderful perfect mixture it would be; time and time after time.

I know that mom did not learn how to cook from her mother. Unfortunately, my grandmother died from the flu when mom was only 12-years-old. I regret I never asked Mom how she learned to cook. If I had, Mom would have looked at me like I had lost my mind, and would have been simply, "Baby, it's just something I just do." I surmise that my mother's cooking abilities grew out of her survival instincts. Having to feed a family with little to no money, she learned very early how to take little bits of this and a pinch of that and stretch the ingredients to feed everyone. That she could do so, while making it tasty was her secret recipe.

Sundays, holidays, special family gatherings were always filled with wonderful memories of all kinds of food. Both Mom and Dad worked very physically demanding jobs; for over thirty-five years mom worked in a glass factory making cardboard boxes used in shipping glasses. Mom would work double shifts, two eight-hour shifts. Shift work meant she worked six days on week one from 7am to 3pm, six days on week two from 3pm to 11pm, followed closely by six more days from 11pm to 7am, then she started this crazy, mixed up cycle all over again. So to be perfectly clear, mom was more often than not working and not at home. Despite her overwhelming demanding work schedule, she made sure we had food ready and waiting for us. Our daily meals included a pot or two of meat, seasoned vegetables, a pot of rice, and from time to time, some form of meat, most likely fried chicken.

Meat served was whatever freshly killed livestock was available, whether from our small farm, caught, captured, hunted in the wild, or given to us by family and friends. Typically, we had chicken, pork, freshly caught fish found at the back door courtesy of a friend, or beef. We often had rabbit hunted by my grandfather, muskrat caught by a neighbor, or deer shot by a family friend. I have hilarious memories about the time we came upon a giant turtle while traveling along on the back two-lane road near our home. Upon seeing the turtle, mom slammed on her brakes, jumped out of the car, grabbed the turtle and tossed it into the trunk of her car. All this occurred within seconds. The next day we had the most delicious turtle soup served with cornbread I have ever tasted.

The overwhelming majority of meat prepared in our home was simmered on the stove top for most of the day, baked for hours, or deep fried in hot oil; always and forever, the meal was always served WELL DONE. We affectionately referred to our meat as being dead, no red blood anywhere. I never ate a steak prepared medium until I was over thirty-years-old. Steak in our house was pounded, drenched in flour, fried in Crisco, and then smothered in gravy and onions. The concept of sautéed meats or vegetables did not exist for us.

Mom and Dad hosted annual September family reunions. These gatherings were the real life version of black family reunions on steroids. Our family would come from all over, at least 100 family members, usually driving for days to gather in our backyard for a weekend of eating, laughing, sharing stories, and loving on each other. Mom's aunties in New York City and Newark would bring their entire families to South Jersey so that they could check on their deceased sister's three daughters and their families. Not only were family members able to eat all they could, but everyone was encouraged to pack a togo dinner for later. All who wanted left with vehicles full of recently harvested fresh vegetables.

At our family gatherings, Mom took great care to make sure the menu included every kind of soul food, including desserts. Mom's main course always included barbecue ribs and blue crabs. Dad and his buddies would slow cook slab after slab of pork ribs all night on the wood fire pit. Some years, the fire pit would feature a whole pig, head, feet and all. No gathering was complete in South Jersey unless it had bushel baskets of live blue crabs that were cooked on an outdoor fire pit in a big black cast iron pot. That black cast iron pot had magical powers; throughout the reunion, no matter how many crabs were eaten, the pot was forever overflowing.

Much to my surprise, I have become my mother and greatly appreciate and understand that food provides nutrition as well as nurturing the soul. As it should be with each new generation, I have continued her legacy and reinforced our love of food, family, and friends. My friends affectionately refer to me as their "B. Smith." Like my mother, food is the focal point of all gatherings in my home. Like my mother, my husband and I have many Sunday gatherings where I prepare multiple main course dishes.

While I am my mother's daughter, I add my own personal touch by creating a theme for each event and providing specialty decorations, upping the experience. One of my most favorite hosted events was the cruised-themed party I gave for my girlfriend's 40th birthday. The entire house, including our three-car garage was converted into a cruise ship. We arranged parking at a nearby church and guests were driven by golf carts to our home where they ascended the red-carpeted gang plank and entered the transformed ship. Greeted by a photographer taking portraits in front of the ice sculptures, guests were then handed the deck plan. The directory included the Dolphin Disco, Welcome To Your Life Photograph Gallery, Place Your Bet Casino, the Havana Cigar Smoking Bar, and Jazz Under the Stars Lounge featuring a live band. The seafood dining experience included food from around the world.

Unlike my mother, I no longer try to cook and prepare all of the food for the larger functions hosted at our home. Many times family and friends are asked to contribute an item or prepare a dish. For the larger gatherings at my home, I rely exclusively on my neighbor, friend, and caterer. I am so thankful that God sent the angel of food to me and she resides right in my neighborhood. In fact, whenever a friend asks to use our home as the venue for their celebration, I ask them to first confirm the food with my neighbor, friend, and caterer. While I am definitely my mom's daughter, I am also a working businesswoman and I have learned to employ the art of delegation. As with my mom, I believe the event cannot happen if the food is not right and my neighbor, friend, and caterer understands the importance of the nurturing the soul through food.

Mom did master the preparation of quite a few dishes and we continue to crave those dishes since her passing. Mom's sweet potato pie is even better than Patty LaBelle's pie. In fact, we would argue that Patty LaBelle copied mom's sweet potato pie recipe. Unequivocally, collard greens were Mom's premiere dish.

Later in life after moving to Atlanta to live with my family, mom prided herself on cooking and serving collard greens to our neighbors and my book club members. The greens were always the super star dish of any meal we had. Mom enjoyed showing all of our family au pairs how to select, clean, wash, and cook collard greens. Our French au pair, Orane, and mom spent hours together in the kitchen preparing pot after pot of collard greens for Sunday dinners and special gatherings. Mom would always affectionately tell Orane that she would surely find a husband if she prepared and served collard greens once she returned to France.

Mom had the knack of telling stories about the past through the meals she ate, and sharing stories of what she ate and when, even if it occurred twenty-five or more years ago. What was so amazing was that these were long forgotten events but she remembered exactly what happened through the food we shared. Mom lived to be ninety-years-old and during her eighties, she showed signs of suffering from loss of short-term memory and displayed signs of dementia. However, Mom's long-term memory was intact. What was so unusual is that Mom could remember what she ate and the food that she was served even if it was decades ago. She was so good at recollecting her eating experiences. Mom could recite the food that was on the menu, how it was prepared, and whether it was good. What an amazing talent to be able to recite what you ate and how it tasted from travels 10 or 15 years ago. My mother and I did not share this same talent. I can barely remember what I ate for breakfast. Nevertheless, my younger son has the gift, and like his grandmother, he can recite what was served or what he ate years later. I think it must be a genetic gene; a condition that manifested in my mom skipped me and reappeared in my younger son.

One of the nicest compliments I received from my mother occurred within a year of her death while sitting at our kitchen table during Sunday dinner. In a whisper, Mom said to my husband that I was a good cook. She continued her compliment with a smile and uttered that my meals were tasty and good even though I did not cook like her. I have availed myself of countless cookbooks, a few cooking classes, and television shows and countless questions at restaurants and have been known to beg friends to share their secrets. What mom did not realize is that I had captured the best of her ingredients, the essence of her cooking, and her gift of nurturing the soul through food.

Even in death, food had a place for my mom and our family. Two weeks prior to her death, mom stopped eating. We spent every hour trying to force food into her. We prepared her most favorite dishes, took her to her preferred restaurants, and ordered all the foods we knew she enjoyed. Much to our dismay, Mom only would eat a couple of spoons of her favorite foods, and then say she was full. My husband and I knew the end was near although we could not say it to each other or anyone else.

On the day mom transitioned, our friends and family surrounded her, each arriving with something for her to eat. My girlfriend, affectionately called mom's "white daughter" because of her light complexion, arrived with her fancy stacked different color and flavor Jell-O. With spoon in hand, mom opened her mouth, took a half spoonful, and smiled. Likewise, our dearest friend's mother arrived with her specialty sweet potato pie with another spoon in hand. Mom was only able to swallow a small portion. We held on to hope and belief that if we could get Mom to eat, that it would permit her to stay here on earth with us a little longer.

Reality came crashing into our revelry when our dearest friend who is a surgeon, whispered to us that we are only feeding the cancer and that the food was not providing the nutrition for her body. Our hearts were broken but we were certain that in those last moments here on earth, Mom needed the food, not for the nutrition but to help us understand that her spirit and soul was entering the next world.

Even after death, food had a place in my mother's life and that of our family. After Mom had transitioned, we had much confusion and laughter centered again on food. Our home was filled with family and friends who had come running to say their final goodbyes to Mom in person. There were over twenty people in our home that Sunday morning. My son came to me and said that he had asked a delivery man from one of the local upscale restaurants to move his truck from the driveway so that the people from the funeral home could drive up to the front door to remove "the body" (my dear Mom). My son handed me a receipt and asked me to sign for a full course dinner that had been set up in the kitchen. I was confused, had someone ordered dinner for us?

As I entered my kitchen, smells of a wonderful Italian meal penetrated the air. Everything was set up on my granite countertop for a feast, arranged in serving trays and chafing dishes and kept warm by burners. As I looked at the young delivery person dressed in his black uniform and studied the address of the invoice, I had to tell him that the food was not for our home but my neighbor. He had delivered and set up the wonderful banquet of food at the wrong house! The delivery person was visibly disturbed not just by the fact that he was at the wrong house, but distressed and totally confused as to why he had to move his van so that the "body" could be taken out. As I stood there, smelling the wonderful smells of Italian food, which by the way my mother loved, all I could do was laugh. Everyone in the kitchen joined me in the laughter because we all could hear my mother saying with passion, "Young man, I'm so sorry this mistake was made but we need to eat some of that food. Don't you see all of our hungry guests? I cannot let them leave this house without eating something. So get me those plates to hand out!"

Home, A Place For Shelter and Love

I made a promise to myself that when I got married and started a family, I would never have anyone but my immediate family under my roof. This promise to myself was grounded in the fact that I grew up in a house full of "characters" whose last names were not the same as my immediate family. Our house was not the traditional mom, dad, a few kids, and a dog. Rather it was Mom, Dad, me and my brothers, the neighborhood drunk, women transitioning from the state mental institution back into society, male teenagers needing foster care, and relatives or whoever was in need of shelter or food who were lucky enough to find our open door. My mom wanted us to believe that all these nefarious groups of people represented business ventures that were contributing to our family income, helping on the farm, or with chores around the house. My dad's unequivocal position was "we just needed to do this."

If my parent's home at RD1 Box 112 in South Jersey had a voice, it would give you the best retrospective view of those early years. And this is what it would tell you...

I was built in the 1950s on a five-acre tract of farmland on the corner of Rogers and Irving Avenues. The tract of land that I stand on was expanded years later to include adjacent 25-acre parcel of prime farmland. Irving Avenues connected the county towns of Millville and Bridgeton in South Jersey. I was your classic ranch-style home, in that wonderful shade of pink that took on other wonderful shades of pink with each new touch-up. I was built to accommodate a family of five, but from the very beginning, it became apparent I was meant to house a village. I lost count very early on, as new faces appeared and took up residence in "the pink house on the corner." People came, stayed, had babies, got married, got on their feet, moved on, and a few died. Let's just say there was never a vacancy, and Leon and Cat liked it that way. All these folks were fed, sheltered, loved, and sent on their way in much better shape than they had arrived, both financially and spiritually.

The family was always hosting a major gathering in the backyard. Adults and children would come from afar and stay for days. There was plenty of laughter, games, and trash talking going on. Cat would constantly yell to the children who ran in and out of my back door to "close the door."

Cat and Leon were forever nurturing and raising a host of children. There were never enough rooms but plenty of beds to accommodate everyone. All of the children that I remember crossing my threshold were blessed with a strong circle of love and encouragement. Night after night, I could hear Cat and Leon engaging with these young minds and teaching them the value of hard work, education, faith, family, and service to others.

The rotation of bodies coming and going lasted for more than five decades until Leon passed on and Cat moved to Atlanta under protest. I remember those late night conversations Cat had on the phone. I overheard her say, "I do not intend to move anywhere. I want to stay in my own home, on my land and farm!" Cat did leave me. At first she would come back often and stay for extended periods of time. As time went on, the periods of absence grew longer.

I stand vacant, waiting for my next family, my rebirth. I am locked, secure, and still have running water, heat, and power. Time has taken its toll on some of my features; my roof leaks and my windows no longer keep that cold northern air out during the winter months. Nevertheless, structurally I stand strong and ready for my next life.

Cat surprised me and returned in the spring of 2016 with her daughter, Cynthia. My rooms have been quiet for some time, she left her about four years for good. Little did I realize that this visit would become the very last that I would hear her voice. I was excited to feel her presence again and to watch as she roamed from room to room, stopping and looking at everything. As she and Cynthia left, I overheard Cat saying much to my dismay, "It's no longer my house." Cynthia said nothing.

Cat died within four months of this visit. I know this is not the end for me within the family estate, but my direction is yet to be determined. I look forward to nurturing many souls and returning to the grand days of a revolving door of residents and countless parties and family gatherings in the backyard; the noise, the laughter, the love!

Let me remind myself and the reader, I made a promise to myself that when I got married and started a family, I would never have anyone but my immediate family under my roof. Much to my dismay, I am my Mom's daughter. I have become her.

If my home could talk, it would tell you...

I sit on land that was considered as being out in the country. Since slavery, I have always been owned by African Americans and to this day many of the homes surrounding me are black-owned. The entire area is now considered to be an in-town neighborhood and prime real estate. When my family decided to move here, I am told it's because they were growing out of the "Alexander Hotel." They had a house to accommodate a family of five – mom, dad, two sons, and a dog. After 12 years, it just wasn't the family homestead Chuck and Cynthia desired for raising a family.

In 1998, I became the Alexander homestead and no longer housed just a family of five. It did not take long for their historical open-door policy to embrace family and friends in need. Like her mom, Cynthia opened my doors to all in need. 1519 was the temporary address for mother-in-laws, cousins, siblings, nieces, nephews, au pairs, and party destinations for birthday celebrations, graduations, wedding events, book clubs, holiday dinners, and family reunions. Like her Mom, Cynthia considered me a place to be shared and to nurture souls.

I am officially known as the party house in the neighborhood. I am the location of smaller family gatherings as well as gatherings with over 100 in attendance. For the larger functions, Cynthia utilized all of my spaces including the backyard. At one function, I overheard a guest ask if the lush green backyard was part of a park or actually part of the house.

Cynthia's mom came and stayed for ten years. She was so very proud of me. Cynthia and she would get into arguments because her mom would take people on tours, showing me off to everyone who agreed to follow her. My rooms were always filled with young kids at first and then later with teenagers hanging out. When originally built there was an alarm system installed but the system is rarely turned on because there is always someone present.

My walls are fairly quiet now that Cynthia's mom has passed and the boys are now grown and live in their own place. I have many vacancies right now but I know it is only a temporary vacancy. Cynthia is in fact her mom and she will invite someone to live with them. How fortunate for me, the tradition continues.

Catherine & Cynthia

Catherine P. Robinson (1926 - 2016)

The Women We Watched

WINFORD "WINNIE" MOON

God bless you Linda! Sonja

By: Sonja Moon Jackson

The women I watched taught our family how to love.

It's not hard for most of us to imagine a time, not so long ago, when many African American women made their daily living by serving others. *The Help*, written by Kathryn Stockett, brought to life the reality of a community of black women who arose each day to serve others as a means to feed their families. And this important, post slavery community of women was commonplace in the South and in many parts of America. My grandmother and mother were no exception to this praxis, and for their numerous sacrifices I'm forever grateful. My grandmother, in all her wisdom, never studied beyond the third grade. Yet she was the wisest, most intuitive, witty, and classiest woman I've ever known. She passed all of these personality traits on to her children, including my mom; and for many generations to come, our family will model her love, grace, compassion, and selflessness.

My grandmother did not take the art of service lightly, meaning she refused to work for poorer clientele, *choosing* only to work for more wealthy clients – doctors, lawyers and other successful professionals. While her selective philosophy was financially motivated, she also witnessed many uneducated and poorer employers mistreat her close friends, in those employers' efforts to bolster their sense of self-importance and gain social status by hiring maids. She catered annual Christmas parties for Dr. Crawford and Dr. Greenly, polished hardwood floors in Attorney Gordon's fine home, and starched shirts from her home for judges and local politicians. I distinctly recall her sharing a story of a birthday party that she catered on a "fine house boat." Her eyes danced as she shared with me how she and her friends created lovely hors d'oeuvres, seafood fritters, hand-held desserts, and petit fours, all served on beautiful silver trays. Similarly, whenever we celebrated a holiday at her modest home, she insisted that we use serving trays for every item. Amazingly, she had the foresight to brand herself in a small town, as the classy "help" of color to hire. In turn, she only allowed her two daughters to work or babysit for the most influential and affluent families in our hometown.

As my grandmother and mom worked in these homes, they were exposed to conversations, mindsets, and the various fine things that many African Americans would otherwise never know, such as quality fabrics and clothing, fine china, beautiful antiques, and pricey rugs. Despite the fact that my grandmother lived in that small, shabby, two-bedroom house on Lake Street, she learned everything that she could from her clients and passed this knowledge on to her children and grandchildren. My grandfather worked for the Brumby Chair Co. in their local factory, so my grandparents' combined income was meager at best. However, when my uncle showed the propensity to be a quantifiable genius, my grandmother cooked, washed, ironed clothes, and cleaned homes to earn enough money to enroll him in boarding school. As a direct result of her tenacity, my uncle graduated from Boggs Academy, later served on their Board of Directors, served in the U.S. military, and worked for years on the International Olympic Committee. There is no greater show of love than when a mother sacrifices in order for her children to have a better life.

My mom and her sister were inspired by my grandmother to reach for the best as well. Despite growing up desperately poor, my mom was a popular cheerleader in high school and was effortlessly recognized as Miss Lemon Street High School. Looking at Mom's sophisticated high school photographs, one would never guess my grandparents' humble earnings. Mom's tea-length dresses were stunningly fashionable, complimented by the appropriate hats and gloves to match. These gorgeous dresses were purchased from the finest stores in town or donated by my grandmother's employers. Regardless, my mom looks stunning in her pictures; and even though she's a beautiful lady, Mom has always remained exceptionally humble and unassuming. (Apparently, these character traits were attractive to my dad, because they began dating in high school and have been married for almost 60 years.) Mom and her sister both finished high school and continued on to nursing and business school. From my perspective, my grandmother's personal stories and trials served to make her children stronger.

However, if you ask Mom about her childhood, her memories are overshadowed by chronic periods of uncertainty, pain, and loss. My grandfather never managed their finances well at all, so there were times when the children would come home from school and the lights would be disconnected. Vivid in Mom's memory is the year when my grandfather failed to pay property taxes, so Mom earned money babysitting and cleaning homes in order to pay their property taxes. Because Mom was forced to deal with adult situations as a young teenager, she developed a sense of tenacity and a strong determination well beyond her years. Just to put this scenario into perspective, can you imagine any sixteen-year-old that you know today who would willingly volunteer to work after school in order to pay their parent's taxes and save their home? Certainly, no teenagers that I know...

As time moved on, my grandfather grew very ill and passed away, and my grandmother moved to public housing. This timeframe serves as the backdrop for the fondest memories from my childhood. Both my grandmothers, paternal and maternal, lived in public housing, and my sister and I would freely roam from one apartment to the other. By the way, despite her limited finances, my paternal grandmother also made social statements in her own right. Not only was she PTA president, but her Bridge Club met every Wednesday. She painted the cement floors of her apartment, kept it spotless, and had the most beautiful burgundy and cream striped Duncan Phyfe sofa in her living room. She loved to call and let us know that she had cooked a batch of her famous vegetable soup; and we'd all gather around her kitchen table where she served us homemade vegetable soup from her beautiful bone china. Interestingly, public housing back in the 50s and 60s was not deemed a kiss of death; but low-income housing served to improve living conditions for many folks who otherwise would be forced to live in substandard housing. Having said this, both of my grandmothers used their influence and lives to reach out to their neighbors who couldn't afford food, and they welcomed and embraced strangers in need. Mom admonished her mother, to no avail, about inviting numerous, inebriated strangers in her home to sleep off their drunken state. It's certain that this was my grandmother's calling – to encourage and inspire her neighbors to live their lives in hope for better days. Literally, it gave her measurable joy to help others. In some cases though, her efforts to reach others commanded her family's involuntary participation. Just one example that comes to mind is when a local bakery discovered that my grandmother was willing to hand out overstocked bread, so they began delivering *loaves and loaves* of bread to her apartment every week. Given that my grandmother never owned a car, her children and grandchildren became her dispatchers, drivers, and delivery staff. This hope that she instilled in others through her own acts of kindness, inspired a woman, who had been a former drug addict to turn her life around. For weeks, she slept on my grandmother's floor at night, while my grandmother encouraged and prayed for her. After the woman turned her life around, she moved to a small town in Alabama; and to this day, this town celebrates a special day honoring my grandmother, and they use this special day as the platform to inspire others to recognize everyday heroes as well as to reach out to those in need.

Storytelling has always been a longstanding tradition for many families; yet as a child, I found it somewhat challenging to be patient as my grandmother reminisced about her childhood and adult memories. In retrospect, I wish I knew then what I know now! Even still, I loved to watch the twinkle in her eyes as my grandmother laughed, and she had the happiest eyes you could ever imagine. She joyfully shared a story proclaiming, "One night my roommate and I had a party up on the rooftop in Canton. We put on our best dresses, and ooooooh, we danced and we danced all night long! I mean that was one of the best times in our lives!" Once when I was a hopelessly in love teenager dating a young man who she didn't approve of, she shared a painful secret memory about her first marriage. She could never pronounce my name, so she lovingly called me "Sanda." "Sanda, I need to tell you something. Did you know that I was married to a young man before I married your granddad?" Perhaps I knew this story, but I couldn't recall the details, so I stood in her bedroom doorway to hear the juice. "I married a young, handsome man whom I loved, and I thought he loved me too. We had one child together before we divorced."

At this point, I'm thinking to myself, *"Wait. What?!?!"*

She continued with her story, "Then one day I was walking along the road on my way to church, and a man rode up to me on a horse and said to me, 'Ida, I need to let you know that your husband has been taken into custody, because he's murdered another man.'"

"Who did Jim kill?" my grandmother softly asked. And the officer informed her that her husband was arrested for the murder of his mistress's husband. My grandmother went on to explain to me how she faced the very public humiliation, shock, and heartbreak in a small town. "The church play was that evening, so I willed myself to that church. By the time I reached the church, the news had spread through town like a wild fire; and as I entered the church, and walked down that aisle, I could hear audible whispers, snickering, and hurtful mocking. But you know what I did? I held my head up high. I said my lines in the play, and I filed for a divorce that week. Your grandmother has been tried by fire many times in my life. But I never let my trials take me over, and always tried to learn from my mistakes. Sanda, I'm telling you all of this, because I can't bear to see my grandchild make the same mistake that I made; and I don't want you to experience the same pain that I had to endure."

When I told my mom what my grandmother shared with me that night, Mom stood in the middle of the floor in complete astonishment, because my grandmother had never shared this story with her or my aunt. The fact that my grandmother felt that I was important enough to reopen her deepest wounds, that changed the course of her life, gave me genuine pause. What a phenomenal way to show her love. Needless to say, I heeded my grandmother's words, and broke it off with the young man who, in some way, must have reminded my grandmother of her ex-husband.

The strength of both my grandmothers, as well as my mother, has always served as a beacon for all of the major decisions in my life. I watched how these loving women made conscious efforts to treat everyone with respect, dignity, and compassion. Whether you were the town's known alcoholic or the town's mayor, you were always welcomed and embraced with open arms. The pastor of our church visited my grandmother for two hours every Sunday, hanging on her every word, laughing at her incessant wit, and he always left with a full belly. Without exception, connecting with youths was their natural passion; and to this day – regardless of race – my high school classmates adore Mom. Recently, on a whim, I posted birthday wishes for Mom on Facebook, and she received almost 200 comments and "likes" celebrating her 75th birthday. Almost predictably, many of the birthday wishes and expressions of adoration came from my high school classmates. Walking in my grandmother's footsteps, Mom has touched so many youths' lives over the years, with her loving words of wisdom, with her kind yet direct admonitions, and thoughtful suggestions. If a troubled youth confided in her about poor decisions that took them down troubled roads, never did she condemn them or rush to judgment. Instead, she offered and still offers kind words, heartfelt encouragement, and challenged the troubled teen to look to The Higher Love for guidance. In return, so many youths have thanked Mom for encouraging and coaching them through tough times in their lives.

I also watched how my mom made thoughtful, well-planned decisions in her own life, carefully weighing pros and cons, before arriving at a conclusion. The little girl who grew up on Lake Street, married her childhood sweetheart, supported her husband's businesses and professional career, raised two daughters, sent her daughters to college, and became the Greatest Grandma in the World to her three adoring grandchildren. That same little girl from Lake Street probably never imagined a world for herself where she would have her own home, travel the world many times over, be free from financial uncertainties, and be confident in both who she "was" as well as who she "was not." That little girl made career choices that allowed her to stay closely involved in my and my sister's school activities, enrolled us in Girl Scouts, ballet, and piano lessons, and paid for college. Nonetheless, make no mistake, the childhood bumps and bruises that Mom endured have made her exceptionally grateful for her blessings, and she makes absolutely no apologies for vowing to never forget from whence she came.

Understandably, this deliberate choice to have gratitude for your own blessings compels you to love others who may or may not look like you. My grandmother rose each day actively searching for ways to express acts of kindness to those whom others may have shunned. Similarly, rather than condemning those less fortunate, Mom continues my grandmother's legacy by looking for ways to encourage the downtrodden, and inspiring them to make that significant turn in their life that will lead their path in a better direction. If anyone wishes to be beloved, the women that I watched would encourage you to look no further than yourself. They would encourage you to possess class without casting judgment. Show compassion in lieu of scoffing at others' failures, and place your neighbor's well being ahead of self-proclaimed importance. Thank you, Mom and Grandma for showing us how to love.

Winford with Walter Moon;
circa 1959

RUBY GENEVA LEEVY JOHNSON

By: Rev. Chris Leevy Johnson, PhD

"WE'VE GOT TO SERVE THESE FAMILIES"

In the fall of 1997, a new employee of Leevy's Funeral Home was complaining that he had to take chairs to a family after he was scheduled to get off work at 6 p.m. His sour attitude and protest offended Miss Ruby (the name commonly used by employees and persons who knew her). Miss Ruby had lived at the funeral home since 1951. Despite the fact that she lived above the funeral home, she got to work every morning between 4 and 5 a.m. after answering the phone all night long. Essentially she worked all day and all night. Although she seldom asserted her authority, as President of the company, this complaint by an employee of Leevy's Funeral Home objecting to serving a family, drew her scorn. She immediately announced in a strong and authoritative voice, "We've got to serve these families."

Ruby Geneva Leevy Johnson was born on February 8, 1917 in Columbia, South Carolina. She was the first child born to Isaac Samuel Leevy and Mary Kirkland Leevy. The Leevys were the parents of four children. In addition to Ruby, there was Isaac Kirkland Leevy, born May 7, 1918; Carroll Moten Leevy, born October 13, 1920; and Marian Naomi Leevy, born in 1922. When she was born in 1917, it was the end of Reconstruction in South Carolina. As a result of Jim Crow laws, a de facto system of apartheid reigned in South Carolina. Segregation was rigidly enforced. Most negroes lived in very well-defined areas. In the case of the Leevy family, the family lived in what was designated as the Ward One section of Columbia. The area was generally identified as Gervais Street on the north; Blossom Street on the south; Assembly Street on the east; and Lincoln Street on the west. It was a close-knit community of negroes. The community was populated with single-family dwellings, churches, and black-owned businesses.

No story of Ruby Geneva Leevy Johnson would be complete without an extensive discussion of her father, Isaac Samuel Leevy. He was her role model. His involvement in business and community activities profoundly impacted her life. She adopted his desire to be of service to others. This one factor more than any other in her life guided her career. Her father, widely known as I.S. Leevy, was one of the state's leading black businessmen. The black business district, in the early nineteen hundreds, was located generally in the Park and Washington Street area of Columbia, about seven blocks from where they lived and two blocks from the white shopping district on Main Street. The family could walk to and from where they lived and worked.

Isaac Samuel Leevy, Jr. was born on May 3, 1876 in the Antioch Section of Kershaw County, South Carolina. He was one of ten children born to Isaac Samuel Leevy, Sr. who was born into slavery and Laura Hunter Leevy, who was born free. A product of poverty, he was determined at an early age to overcome the circumstances of his environment. He was educated in the public schools of Kershaw County and graduated from Mather Academy in Camden, South Carolina. Mather Academy was a private institution for the privileged. Because the Leevy household had meager resources, his parents did not have enough money to pay the dollar a month tuition. Mr. Leevy put himself through school. He found odd jobs cutting wood and other chores in the community to fund his education.

"As I grew older and visualized my desperate, poverty-stricken condition, I could see no remedy unless I could get away from home to school. I persuaded my father to let me go to Mather Academy (Browning Home) in Camden, South Carolina, about ten or twelve miles from my home. After much worry, because there was no way in the world to get a dollar to pay tuition and to pay for the needed books, I in some way was able to get a dollar; and my father went to Camden and paid the dollar for a month's tuition."

Leevy recalled that excelling at Mather was very difficult because of his impoverished condition. The other boys in his classes came from prominent families, and he was from a small poor community. Some of them teased him for his poor dress, but he was determined to succeed and excel.

A careful examination of the family reveals that working and serving others were core values of the family. Mr. Leevy opened a tailoring shop business soon after he moved to Columbia. It was a very successful business. It was patronized by black and white customers. At the turn of the century, tailor-made suits were in vogue. Mr. Leevy's tailoring skills distinguished him as one of the best tailors in the city. He used the business to train other tailors. He also used the business to instill in his family members a work ethic. In 1917, Mr. Leevy opened Leevy Department store at 1131 Washington Street in Columbia as an outgrowth of his tailoring business. It became the largest black-owned dry goods store in the state. The department store featured a tailoring shop, barbershop, beauty salon, and a dressmaking department. Even though the department store was opened primarily to sell ready-made clothes, Mr. Leevy maintained the tailoring business. He understood that as a result of the growing ready-made clothes market, tailoring would become extinct especially among negro consumers. Mindful of this possibility, nevertheless, with his affiliation with the National Business League, he encouraged other tailors to remain vigilant in their craft despite the changing economic climate. Mr. Leevy stated, "The greatest handicap comes in making and fitting at prices that will compete with the cheap agencies that are carrying the crowd and putting the negro tailor out of business and driving him away from the trade." In 1925, Mr. Leevy had 17 employees. Because of his entrepreneurial prominence, he was elected president of the local chapter of the Negro Business League. In 1926, the local branch had 46 members. Mr. Leevy was instrumental in helping other negro businesses get started and survive.

A family member who was one of his best students; his daughter, Ruby. She performed every task assigned her as soon as she was old enough and able to work. Her father was a demanding taskmaster. He believed in hard work and he expected everyone to follow his example. No one was exempt from working in the family businesses. Since he was such a successful entrepreneur, his business enterprise afforded his children unlimited opportunities to learn various skills and to be productive. This included keeping records, counting revenue, secretarial assignments, as well as maintenance work such as sweeping, dusting, and stocking products. His daughter Ruby excelled at all these duties. What would be described as menial duties where tackled with diligence and duty. The lessons she learned helped structure her life. She became a workaholic. She was not a clock-watcher. She devoted full time to any job she held. This was even evident when she was a teenager. While attending elementary and high school, not only did she excel academically, she also worked practically every afternoon and on weekends performing chores at one of her father's businesses. She continued working with her parents in the department store until her father became the first black ESSO franchise owner in the state of South Carolina in 1928. The gas station was located at the corner of Taylor and Gregg Streets. When Mr. Leevy opened the Leevy Gas Station, my grandmother was 13-years-old and a student at the Howard Colored School. The next year she would attend the city's first segregated high school for negroes: Booker T. Washington High School, also founded by her father. Mr. Leevy was a contemporary of the Wizard of Tuskegee, Booker T. Washington whom the school was named after.

When Mr. Leevy came to Columbia in 1907, there was only one public school for colored children living in the City of Columbia, namely Howard Colored School. It was named after General Oliver Otis Howard (i.e. Howard University) a Union General who helped liberate the South. The school was located across the street from the Richland County Jail in the 800 block of Hampton Street. Mr. Leevy was motivated by a belief in the importance of an education, and a desire to obtain a good education for his children motivated him to seek to try and organize another school for colored children residing in Columbia. With the cooperation of Joseph Pelot, a white citizen who was instrumental in city politics, they petitioned the City of Columbia Board of Education for the construction of a new school within the city limits. There was plenty of opposition to the request, but Mr. Leevy and Mr. Pelot were steadfast in their determination to get approval for the new school. After many setbacks, Mr. Leevy recalled learning one morning by reading an article in the local newspaper. "On a bright morning the daily paper, with large headlines, announced that a site in the Old McCrary Pasture had been purchased by the City Board of Education for a second very much needed school in Columbia for Negroes." That same day Mr. Leevy and Mr. Pelot went to the superintendent's office to thank him and the board for seeing and acting upon the need to construct a new school building for colored students.

The new high school for negroes was completed in 1916. Prior to its completion, the superintendent called Mr. Leevy to solicit a suggestion for the name of the high school. Mr. Leevy replied, "remembering my great friend and brother alumnus, Booker T. Washington," he stated, "I could suggest no better name for the new school." Mr.

Leevy smiled broadly on the day for the laying of the cornerstone proclaiming the establishment of Booker T. Washington High School. This was a significant achievement for negroes in the history of Columbia. Mr. Leevy's mission to get sufficient classrooms for colored children in Columbia did not stop with the Booker T. Washington School. Because of the increase in the black population in the city, a third school was desperately needed. White citizens in the inner city began to move to the suburbs in the 1920s in Wales Gardens and Shandon. One community, which they deserted was the Waverly Community. The Waverly School, therefore, was left vacant when all of the white families living around the school left. Mr. Leevy petitioned the school board to allow the colored citizens of the city to use the six-room school for the educational advancements of the negro citizens in the city. The night before the school board met to discuss the Waverly School adjustment, many of Leevy's supporters called him to say that they would not appear with him at the meeting. He notes in his memoirs that the reneging participants feared white backlash and being fired from their jobs if they went with him. Because Leevy was self-employed and had a mostly black clientele, he had no fear. When he arrived at the school board, the white secretary of the board came out to the lobby to try to talk him out of bringing the petition before the board. He claimed that he feared whites in the city would rather see the school burned down than have colored children in it. Mr. Leevy, with tears in his eyes, answered: "Our understanding is that you were elected to serve both races and our disappointment now is that you are denying our rights to petition under the Bill of Rights and the Constitution of the United States. However, we wish to advise and impress upon you and your board that our people's interest is the education of their children in such that we have no more fear of a stick of dynamite than we have of a stick of candy." The Board meeting was held in February (no year is mentioned) and by September of that year, the school was opened for the colored children of Columbia.

Mr. Leevy, known throughout the community as a fighter for the educational rights of the colored citizens of Columbia, lobbied for more educational facilities for Negro children. In July of 1936, a Miss Charlotte Jackson informed Mr. Leevy that a large group of children in the Kendall Town suburb (where C.A. Johnson High School is currently located) of Columbia had no school to attend. With the help of another lady in the community, Mrs. Harris, (no first name is given) a petition was signed by 263 families claiming that their children had no access to public school education. After meeting again with the secretary of the school board and then the Chairman of the School Board, the board promised that if the colored community would provide the land and a thousand dollars towards the project, the school board would provide a fourth school for colored students. After finding the site, a six-classroom school was built. During a committee meeting about naming the school, a black citizen recommended that the school should be called the Jackson-Leevy Graded School. However, Miss Jackson withdrew her name and the school board named the new school the Leevy Graded School. Miss Jackson became the first principal. When the school was moved to another location near C.A. Johnson High School, it was renamed Carver Elementary School after George Washington Carver.

The majority of schools that Mr. Leevy helped organize and establish in Columbia, South Carolina where named after African American businessmen. Mr. Leevy believed, like Booker T. Washington, that African-American (negro) uplift was contingent on business ownership in the black community. While he was actively engaged in community service, he continued to grow his business empire. While he was in the department store business, Mr. Leevy ventured into two more businesses. One was an Esso Gas Station, which he opened in 1928, and the other was a commercial hog farm located off Highway 555 (now Farrow Road) in 1930[1]. Mr. Leevy opened up the gas station, the first black-owned gas station in the state because, "nowhere in Columbia and probably the state were negroes engaged in the filling station business. With the aim of exploring into this type of enterprise, I moved my house from a corner lot and built in its place Columbia's first filling station owned and operated by a negro."[2] Not only was the colored-owned filling station the first of its kind, it became the nexus for civic activity and a haven for black travelers. Nowhere else in town could black commuters gain access to clean restrooms, cold drinks, and good conversation. Mr. Leevy advertised in the Palmetto Leader that he had an around-the-clock wrecker service and the "Leevy's Better Battery Service."

To expand services to customers, Mr. Leevy started providing a full-time mechanic to repair cars and pump gas. One of his employees and head mechanic was Ollie James Johnson. He was recognized as one of best mechanics in Richland and Fairfield Counties. He not only performed mechanic work, he also taught automobile mechanics at Booker T. Washington High School and at a trade school in Jenkinsville, South Carolina. In 1935, he and my grandmother married. To this union, five children were born, namely, Jamescina, Charles, Carroll, Isaac, and Andrena.

My grandmother and all of her siblings were a major part of every venture my great-grandfather began. This was especially true when he decided to go into the funeral business in 1932. Although she had

---

1 He opened up the hog farm to raise hogs and other vegetables that were taken to the State Farmers Market. He used the food from all of the local hospitals to feed the hogs. According to his daughter, Ruby Leevy Johnson he opened up the hog farm "to make some money." Ruby Leevy Johnson, interview by author, Columbia, South Carolina, December 4, 2003.

2 Ruby Leevy Johnson, interview by author, Columbia, South Carolina, December 12, 2000.

successfully helped perform various tasks in all of his businesses, her true calling was discovered when her father went into the funeral business. This allowed her a platform to show her passion and unique skills to serve the public. She performed various roles. On one occasion someone remarked, "Miss Ruby can do everything except embalm." She never attended a school of mortuary science, however, she did become a licensed funeral director by serving a one-year apprenticeship under her father and successfully passing a written exam. Although she never received any formal training as a funeral director, she certainly could perform any task needed at the funeral home. She could perform secretarial and booking duties; she could wait on families; she could go on funerals to aid families; she played the piano for all chapel funerals, she answered the phone day and night, but most of all she was available to do whatever was needed to make sure families received superior service.

The original funeral home was located inside the Esso Gas Station that my great-grandfather founded in 1930. Originally, her family lived in a two-story home right next door to the funeral home. The gas-station-funeral home was replaced in 1951 with the structure that currently serves as the funeral home. The "corner" served as the center of activity for the Leevy family and my grandmother's family. Not only was it the center of my family's universe, it also became the center of black political might in South Carolina. My grandfather created the Lincoln Emancipation Club to teach blacks how to vote, use a voting machine, and pass illegal voting tests. Furthermore, different groups would use the chapel in the funeral home as a meeting place. Mr. Leevy would later serve on the Board of Directors for the Southern Christian Leadership Conference organized in 1957 by the Reverend Dr. Martin Luther King, Jr., and my great-grandfather was one of the board. Dr. King had refreshments in the family's living room before speaking at the Township Auditorium during the Civil Rights Movement.

Although she and her husband maintained a residence in the Carver Heights section of Columbia, most everyone was in and out of the residence on Gregg Street, especially my grandmother and my father. My grandmother used the Gregg Street residence to provide meals for her parents. When the new funeral home was built, it was designed with two apartments known as the living quarters. One apartment was to be used by my great-uncle, Isaac K. Leevy's family. The other apartment was to be used by my great-grandparents. A room in my great-grandparents area had been set aside for my father. When planning for the construction of the funeral home, my great-grandparents expressed a desire for one of the grandchildren to come live with them and my father; Mr. Leevy's namesake was selected.

While my great-grandparents owned and operated the funeral home, they were heavily dependent on my grandmother. My great-grandfather was blind for most of his life and it was my grandmother's lot to care for her aging parents. She cared for her parents while raising her five children and finishing college at Benedict College. Everyone contributed to their welfare, but it was my grandmother who sacrificed for them the most. She was determined to help them in any way she could but also to make sure the family funeral business succeeded. She was on call 24 hours a day and seven days a week. Although my grandmother had a heavy load of responsibilities with her parents and her duties at the funeral home, in 1957 she decided to return to college to get a college degree. She enrolled in Benedict College and received a Bachelor of Arts degree in 1960, with a major in English. She took courses to become a teacher but after graduating from Benedict she returned to working at the funeral home. She continued to perform the duties that kept her busy day and night.

My great-grandfather died on December 3, 1968. By that time, my father, my grandmother's fourth child, had completed mortuary science school at the University of Minnesota; received a Bachelor of Science degree from Benedict College; awarded a Juris Doctor degree from the University of South Carolina; and had received his license to practice law in the State of South Carolina. Although he was licensed to practice law, after passing the bar he elected to return to work with his grandfather. His first love was the funeral business. My great-grandfather had a succession plan in mind but never put it on paper. He wanted his son Kirk to maintain the business until his grandson and namesake was mature enough to run it. He truly believed that his blood family should carry on the business for generations to come.

When Mr. Leevy died in 1968, the business was left in a family trust. What no one knew until his death was that his wife Mary owned half of the business as well. Mrs. Mary Leevy left her shares to her nine grandchildren and Mr. Leevy left his shares to his three children. So essentially every relative was now a part owner. He named his youngest son, Dr. Carroll M. Leevy, as trustee. Dr. Leevy was an internationally recognized liver specialist, but he had no knowledge of the funeral business and, complicating the matter, he lived in New Jersey. Because of his demanding schedule, he appointed my father and a loyal employee, Claude A. McCollom, as co-managers. This arrangement existed for around two years. Even though my dad and Mr. McCollom were on paper co-managers, my uncle Kirkland tried to run the show. Recognizing the splintering of authority, my dad decided to open a law firm. Even though there was familial turmoil, my grandmother remained faithful to her father's business. She was unwavering in her commitment to the business. She was also in total support of her son's decision to enter the practice of law. As a matter of fact, she became his first secretary. In addition to fulfilling her responsibilities at the funeral home, from 9 a.m. to 4 p.m. she worked in his law office to support him. Clients calling his office would sometimes hear her answer the phone, "Leevy's. I'm sorry I. S. Leevy Johnson law firm." She normally answered the phone at the funeral home by simply saying "Leevy's."

After the tragic death of Isaac Kirkland Leevy in 1970, the funeral home was purchased by his son and daughter, Greg and Glory Leevy. My dad was practicing law full time and was in the State House Legislature and no other family member worked at the funeral home. At that time, my grandmother had been living upstairs in the funeral home for the past two years. Just like all of the persons who managed the business after her father died, she remained loyal and supportive of her nephew and niece. She continued to perform important roles but her most important job was to answer the phone at night. Leevy's has never used an answering service and, I might add, never will. Having an employee answer the phone was always a key ingredient to the operation of the business. When my great-grandfather was alive, he answered the phone 24 hours a day. He used this procedure to keep abreast of all pertinent developments. Also, he used it to skillfully manage the business. Nothing occurred at the business that he did not know about and control. My grandmother carried on this tradition. However, she never tried to exercise any management control of the business during the tenure of her nephew and niece.

Her nephew and niece owned the business from 1970 to 1995. When my great-grandfather died, Leevy's was the leading African American funeral home in Richland County. More families were served by Leevy's than any of its competitors. During the period that her nephew and niece owned the business, the business gradually declined. The poor performance of the business caused the trustee, Dr. Leevy, to institute action to repossess the business. The case finally ended up in bankruptcy court. An attorney was appointed to restructure the business or sell it. During the interim, my father, I. S. Leevy Johnson, and his cousin, Gloria Y. Leevy, were appointed co-managers. Both of them had grown up in the living quarters of the funeral home. They were raised like brothers and sisters. However, the dispute caused estrangement. Eventually the bankruptcy court ordered the funeral home to be sold to the highest bidder. My father was the highest bidder. He became owner of the funeral home on June 15, 1995.

Five years before he purchased the funeral home, I was honored to have been asked by U. S. Senator Fritz Hollins to serve as a United States Senate Floor Page. Because my term did not start until July 1st, I had a month of idle time. For the past six summers and even during the school year, I had worked at the law firm. But, for some reason that I do not know, I asked my cousins if I could spend the month working at the funeral home and I literally fell in love with the funeral business. I will humbly admit I enjoyed going on funerals and having everyone call me Little Leevy! I enjoyed being there every day and working alongside my grandmother and feeling the respect that my family garnered in our community. My grandmother served so many roles. Because she stayed at the funeral home, she answered the phones every night. She had a peculiar way of answering the phone, simply answering the phone and saying "Leevy's" which she stretched out for a good three minutes. Then she went up an octave when she stretched out that second syllable. When I arrived at 9 a.m., she was already at her desk typing and answering the phone. By 1990, the funeral home had computers and an active database to keep up with files and accounts. My grandmother, however, kept her own records and ledgers. She had a memory like an elephant and could remember a case and a balance before the bookkeeper could turn on her computer. She also had a special place on the back of every file where she would record other family members we had served who were relatives of the current deceased. Sometimes, she would have ten to fifteens names of relatives she knew we had buried. Even though I called her Grandma, everyone at the office and in the community called her Miss Ruby. Miss Ruby went on every funeral. When she saw the casket being rolled to the hearse, she went to her seat in the hearse. No matter the temperature, she would patiently wait in the hearse, windows rolled all the way up until the funeral was ready to leave. Once we arrived at the funeral, she would find her seat on the back row of the family side and just sit there (in her later years she slept during the entire funeral).

When I started working at the funeral home in 1990, my grandmother was 73-years-old. I never saw my grandmother make funeral arrangements, drive a car, walk in a family, push out a casket, or dismiss a tent, but her presence made the funeral a LEEVY funeral. Almost everyone who entered the funeral home would acknowledge her presence and search her out. She never got out of the hearse at the cemetery, but all of her friends would come over to the window and pay their respects. And many of them would come over to tell her "Thank you" for something that she had sent them. Ruby Leevy Johnson kept Hallmark Cards in business. My grandmother sent out birthday cards, Christmas cards, Mother's Day cards, Happy Anniversary Cards, graduation gifts, and jokingly even Halloween cards to everyone she knew. If she noticed you were not at a funeral and she thought you should have been there, she would mail you a program. Even when I started working at the funeral home full time and we shared an office, she would still buy stamps and mail me cards. If she saw your name in the delinquent tax notice she would cut your name out of the newspaper and send it to you, not to be funny or embarrass you, but because she cared enough to let you know you needed to go pay your taxes so you didn't lose your house! She really cared!

During my sophomore year at the University of North Carolina, Chapel Hill, I decided that I was no longer going to law school to become a lawyer like my father and brother. But I was gonna become a funeral director. I too, had noticed how horribly my cousins had managed the business and it had become an embarrassment to be known as a Leevy. I called my dad one Sunday night in October of 1993 and told him we needed to buy the funeral home from our cousins and restore its glory! For two years we tried in vain to negotiate with our cousins and we even started looking for property to open up our own funeral home. As fate would have it, they defaulted on a bank loan, the business went into bankruptcy and my father purchased the business in 1995. It was my father's first goal to gain back the community's trust and respect: "I view my goal as coming in and repositioning the funeral home. I view it as just a continuation of the family business. All of us have been connected with the funeral home for over 30 years."

But Ben Piper, the newly appointed manager had loftier goals: "My goal now is to get the funeral home back to being the top funeral home in the state volume-wise, to give superior care and understanding to make it a people-oriented business again. I. S. Leevy was about helping people and not about money."

With his political, academic, and possible judicial service behind him, my dad then focused on his true calling in life: being the owner and director of Leevy's Funeral Home. I. S. Leevy Johnson was able to reposition the business as the leading funeral home in Columbia by demonstrating a complete commitment to superior funeral service and community involvement. As a prominent criminal attorney, he already had visibility. But he had to turn that visibility into a trust and to convince people that the business had a new vision. He quickly remodeled the funeral home, bought a new fleet of cars, landscaped Lincoln cemetery, and purchased uniforms for the staff. These were visible signs that the business was undergoing a complete facelift. He and Ben Piper began attending church meetings and community events to broadcast the new changes at Leevy's. Johnson also subscribed to his grandfather's belief in helping people. He never turned away a family because they could not afford a funeral. And by his side the entire time was his mother and my grandmother, Miss Ruby.

I graduated from the University of North Carolina in May of 1996 and enrolled in mortuary school in Atlanta in August of 1996. I would become the fourth generation of licensed funeral directors in 1998. I will never forget when I started making funeral arrangements in 1999; I forgot to call an organist for a chapel funeral. I knew my grandmother used to be the funeral home pianist and she had played for her church, First Nazareth Baptist Church, which was merely six blocks from the funeral home. But now she was eighty-two-years-old and hadn't played in years. I didn't realize until the family was about to march into the chapel that I forgot to call an organist to play and sing during the funeral. She told me that she hadn't played in years but I told her, "Grandma, I need you." So she grabbed a hymn book and got on the piano.

As soon as she started singing, "What a Friend we have in Jesus" all out of key, the hymn book fell off the ledge and banged off the keys and my grandma yelled out "OOPS!" A grief ridden bereaved family couldn't help but laugh, and my grandmother saved my rear end. Once again, Miss Ruby demonstrated that, "We've got to serve these families."

My grandmother always had my back. From babysitting me to buying me a hot dog on out of town funerals, she always looked out for me. Before my sophomore year, I decided my freshmen year of college at the University of North Carolina that I wanted to become a college professor and teach African-American history. It wasn't until my sophomore year that I decided to also go to mortuary school. After graduating from UNC in 1996, I enrolled in the Gupton College of Funeral Service in Atlanta, Georgia. On the day of my graduation, my classmates voted me as the Bill E. Pierce Award Winner, which went to the graduating senior that best exemplified the essence of funeral service. When they called my name, I was in complete shock. And before I could stand up to go on stage to receive the reward, my grandmother, all four feet, eight inches of her was standing tall, proud of her grandson's accomplishment. Two days after graduating from mortuary school, I enrolled in a PhD program at the University of South Carolina in history. Going to school and working full time was extremely taxing. During the week of midterms and finals I would need to take weeks off at a time. When my dad and other employees would complain, she would defend me and come to my aide and tell them, "You ain't got no degree: THESES are hard!"

My grandmother made an indelible impression on our family, our funeral business, and the entire Midlands of South Carolina. Her commitment to serving families is still the standard we attempt to uphold every day. Like her father, she knew every family we served by name. When they walked through the door she knew them and everyone else in the family we had buried. There was never a time where I have ever known her to clock in sick. She worked every day until her health began to fail her at the age of 92. When I noticed my grandmother slowing down, I asked the Lord to keep her alive until she saw at least one of my children born. I am the youngest of her nine grandchildren and I wanted her to at least see her last great-grandchild born. The Lord answered my prayers when my daughter Leah Denise was born on July 19, 2011. Grandma would go home to be with the Lord on March 5, 2012. She was not physically present when my son, Ian Samuel Leevy Johnson "Little I.S." was born providentially on May 3, 2013. She would have been the first to notice that Little I.S. would share the same birthday as the first I.S. Five years since her passing, we still have her portrait prominently displayed in various rooms in the funeral home as a physical expression of her spiritual presence. Seeing her picture every day is a constant reminder that we must "serve these families."

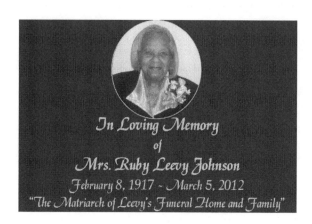

Ruby Leevy Johnson
(1917 - 2012)

MARGARET DELORES BROWN WILSON

By: Tonja Brown

As a child, I was always surrounded by family. There wasn't a major life event that we didn't share together, whether it was a time of celebration or bereavement. My parents often hosted family gatherings, which were filled with great food, good music, and lots of laughter. I have fond memories of visiting family members and hanging out with my cousins. Without saying a word, my parents taught us the importance of family by the life that they lived. As an adult, I have a better appreciation of where this close-knit family approach was born. You see my mom, Margaret Delores Brown Wilson, was born at home on November 14, 1946 on Bogard Street in Charleston, South Carolina. Her parents, Annabell Brown Turner and Julius T. Dingle were never married. My grandmother so loved her baby girl. Despite not having her father present in her life growing up, my mother loved her father and as an adult would have the opportunity to connect with him before his passing. My mother is the oldest of all of her parents' children. My maternal grandmother had three younger children and later in life my mother learned that her father also had three younger children. Marty, as she was affectionately called, was raised in the home with her mother, maternal grandmother, Lula Manigault Brown, and her mother's younger brothers – her uncles Joseph Brown and Eddie Brown who were five years and eight years older, respectively. While Marty was still a young child, her mother, the oldest of her siblings, went to work in New York where employment opportunities were more abundant; she sent money home to care for her family. At an early age, Marty began helping with washing clothes and even missed school to ensure household duties were completed. As a teenager, Marty was responsible for preparing dinner for the family as she closely followed the directions of her grandmother. During the summer her mother would return to Charleston. Annabell married Albert Grant and they had two children - Patricia (five years younger than Marty) and Albert Grant, Jr. (eight years younger than Marty). This marriage ended in divorce. Years later, Annabell fell in love with and married James Turner and the union resulted in one child, Pamela, who was 15 years younger than Marty. Her younger cousin Paula (whose father was Annabell's younger brother, Paul Brown) also came to live with the family in Charleston.

The church I got married in, Central R.M.U.E. Church, located in Charleston, South Carolina became a staple in their life. Marty would take her younger siblings and cousin to Sunday school and then after church she would begin preparing Sunday dinner. Sometimes during the summer months, Marty and her siblings traveled to New York to be with their mother. The close relationship between Marty and her grandmother, who she called Mama, shaped the person she is today. She often recalls the many lessons her grandmother taught her, many routed in her faith and belief in God. Although offered the opportunity to attend college by her mom and James Turner, her stepfather, upon graduating from Burke High School in 1965, Marty followed in her mother's footsteps and traveled to New York to work. Attending college locally would have meant returning home on the weekends to care for her siblings and Marty was looking to be free of those responsibilities. She lived in the Bronx, New York with her Uncle Eddie and his wife, Christine who assumed the apartment that Marty's mom lived in prior to her returning home to Charleston. Marty loved math and initially worked with her Aunt Mildred Martinez, her mom's younger sister, at a watch manufacturing company. She then took a job working with her uncles Joe and Eddie at Howard Printing, and for a change of pace, she took a job as a cashier at Carter's department store.

In 1966, Marty's neighbor, Edna "Ditta" Williams had a dinner party and her guests included both Marty and Ditta's co-worker, Herbert Eugene Wilson, Jr. from the post office. That was how my parents met and they started dating after that night. On December 31, 1966 Marty and Herbert, ages 20 and 24, were joined in holy matrimony in the church Marty attended in Manhattan surrounded by family and friends. Ojetta Harper, Marty's cousin, served as the maid of honor and Willie Smalls served as the best man. Ojetta would later become my godmother and Willie became my brother's godfather. The two lived at 700 East 161 Street in the Bronx, New York, the same home her mother lived in and that my mom once shared with her uncle and his wife. Marty and Herbert later moved to a brownstone at 106 West 113th Street, New York, NY in the same building as her aunt Mildred. The building was just blocks away from Central Park. While reading the newspaper, Marty's husband noticed an advertisement for employment exams for the NYC Transit Authority and encouraged Marty to consider taking the exam. Marty passed the exam and started in payroll and worked with NYC Transit in various roles until 1994 when she decided to take an early retired at age 48, with over 20 years of service. The Wilsons were blessed with two children, Antoine LaMarr in 1968 and Tonja Yvette in 1971 (that's me). With young children, the Wilsons purchased a home and moved to 174-10 126th Avenue, Jamaica, New York. This is the place that I grew up and called home. In 1994, the year that I got married, they moved into a home that they built in Awendaw, South Carolina, a small town approximately 30 miles from where Marty was born and raised. This is also the hometown of Marty's grandmother, Lula Manigault Brown. They live on an acre of land purchased from Marty's mother and stepfather for $1.

There is a saying, "A family that prays together, stays together." Well my family must have done some praying because there was a lot of staying together. There was a sense of responsibility and account- ability for supporting family members. We are family and we help each other, perhaps an unspoken motto, demonstrates that love is an action word. My mother was fortunate to grow up in a loving home sur- rounded by family members, with uncles who were more like big broth- ers and younger siblings that looked up to her. My mother always says that God blessed her and she tries to bless others. This would explain why several family members lived with my parents in the Manhattan brownstone for various periods of time. Perhaps it's difficult for one to truly reflect on the guidance and support that they've received over their life from others and not have a desire to in some way do their part to extend the same loving hand. I would say that generosity is anoth- er lesson that I've learned from watching my parents. I have a saying, "Blessed to be a blessing;" it is a declaration for how I try to live my life and it is reflective of what I see in my mom and dad.

There's a poem that truly inspired me as a parent, "Children Learn What They Live" by Dorothy Law Holte. At some point I became owner of the book by the same title, with the subtitle, *Parenting to In- spire Values* coauthored by Rachel Harris. I have shared the poem with many expecting and new parents. When I receive compliments on my parenting, I am reminded of the many lessons that I learned from watching my mother. I am not sure if my mother ever read this classic poem or the book, but she has embraced many of the key learnings. I am sure that she learned sitting at the feet of her grandmother, in- tently listening as Mama Lula shared the wisdom she gained through her life's experiences. As I reflect on the changing times in America's history, I also realize that my great grandmother, grandmother, and mother did not have access to the tools that I have. So much of their learning came from treasured stories passed down through the gener- ations and testimonies shared by faithful believers. It's not impossible to become a confident and positive woman or loving mother without a good example to follow, but it is certainly advantageous to have foot-steps in the sand to guide you as you travel on the journey of life. Mom and I were both blessed to have wonderful examples of great women to follow.

Loving Mother

My earliest memories of being my mother's daughter are really not memories but stories and pictures that have been shared throughout the years. There is a picture of me as a toddler in a choir uniform. Several family members, including my older brother and cousins and I were a part of a local choir called the Regina Singers, even though I can't sing. I don't actually remember being with the group but my mom has shared lots of stories of our time with the group. One of the fondest of these stories is of me asleep on my mother's lap during a rehearsal and as they started to sing, I awoke, got up off her lap, stood beside the choir director, and begin to join him in directing the choir. Perhaps I knew that singing wasn't my gift but I had the ability to lead. When my mother recounts this memory, there is such joy and pride in her voice and eyes. I see her love for me. This brings me to a picture of the two of us and makes me think of the saying that "a picture is worth a thousand words." In the picture, we are in our apartment at 106 W. 113th Street in the Bronx and there are lots of family members. I am wearing red and white plaid pants and a white turtleneck top and apparently dancing. My mom is just looking at me, with a look that says, "that's my baby." Her eyes, facial expression, and body language say so much. I see how much she loves me. As a mother, I pray that my children see me looking at them with a similar look; the look of a mother's love, a look that says, "I love you with all my heart. You are mine and I am proud of you." These are the words that I hope our pic-tures say. This reminds me that I'll have to spend more time capturing candid shots in addition to those posed pictures that I love so much.

An Involved Parent

She was always there. My mother always encouraged me and supported me with anything that I wanted to do. When I was around nine-years-old, I wanted to go to dance school and she enrolled me in Gloria Jackson Dance Studio. I remember having class every Saturday morning during the season (September to May) until I was older and classes were on Friday evenings. My mom made sure I had everything I needed including leotards, costumes, ballet, tap, and jazz shoes, and she drove me to class. Then at the end of the season, we had recital and my mom invited all of our family members. Then in junior high school, I joined the Girl Scouts. Guess who chaperoned our camping trip and who served as cookie mom? Yes, you guessed right. My mom did all of that! I was a pretty good student, generally well behaved (I was known to speak my mind – blaming this one on Mom and I could be a little talkative), and did well academically. My mom or dad always attended my parent-teacher conferences. I recall one of my high school teachers saying, "It's a pleasure to meet you and thanks for being here. Tonja is doing very well and I wish I had more students like her. I also wish I had more parents like you that showed up and showed support. It seems that the parents that really need to be here aren't." I have three very active children and of course, my husband and I attend parent-teacher conferences, are active in the Parent Teacher Association, have served as coach of our children's teams, as school volunteers, and we make sure they are supported and chauffeured to their extra-curricular activities. We are supporters and advocates of our children. My son, now a college student, realizes the sacrifices we've made for him but reminds me that I did too much. It may require him becoming a parent to truly understand. My mom displayed a level of involvement that I want to replicate with my own children. I am so thankful for her presence, support, and active involvement in our lives.

Working Woman

Every business day, my mom got up and went to work. She'd come home from work and prepare dinner. Early Saturday mornings were reserved for house cleaning before any playing went on and on Sunday we started the day by going to church. I was not familiar with what my mom did professionally but her dedication was evident and she always dressed well and carried herself professionally. She seemed to balance work and home with her very own system. We would go grocery shopping on Saturday morning once a month, traveling to Pathmark grocery store about 20 minutes away. There were grocery stores a lot closer but likely going a little further out provided better quality and more options. Mom would keep a grocery list, clip coupons, and was always aware of whether or not she was getting a good deal on the groceries. I've grown to make my own decisions in life but as my study of human behavior in college has taught me, my decisions to buy Tide detergent and clip coupons are largely influenced by what I saw my mom do. Sometimes we'd travel to a meat market, which, according to Mom provided the best and freshest meat. Perhaps it was because of her love for math and numbers, but mom worked to carefully manage the household bills. All of these may seem simple and routine, however, as a working woman my mom had to balance all the things that had to be done for her family to make a house a home. I was so blessed to never wonder where my next meal would come from or if we'd have groceries to eat because Mom made it happen. Our routine trips to purchase groceries were fun times we shared. My brother and I helped where we could to lighten the load. My mom was a workingwoman, both in the home and outside of it. She is now enjoying retirement from New York City transit but continues to work in the home. Her financial decisions and wisdom as a workingwoman have afforded her a comfortable retirement that has now exceeded the years she worked. What a blessing!

I recall as college students my brother and I visited my mom's place of employment during one of our Christmas breaks. Mom spoke to and greeted everyone with a smile. It seemed that everyone knew my mom, no matter his or her race, gender, or role. "Hey, Marty" rang out with lots of energy. They were as excited to meet us as she was proud to introduce her college children. At work, she had several "adopted children" and they all spoke about how she looked out for them and was always willing to help them. If you sniffled or coughed around my mom, she'd offer you some of her homemade cough medicine, a recipe that was shared with her and that she gladly passes on. My mom had garnered the respect and admiration of her co-workers. When we met her manager and her manager's manager, they went on and on about how wonderful and essential she was to the team. I may not have been able to quite describe what kind of work my mom did but I could tell you that she made a difference in the work that she did. When I got married, my mother's manager gave me a beautiful statue. It is more than a piece of art, it represents for me my mother's impact on her work environment. She made a difference for everyone she came into contact with as she brought sunshine to the situation. My mom was a diligent worker and operated with a spirit of excellence, she gave friendly and warm greetings and a listening ear to her co-workers. As a believer of Jesus Christ, the Son of God, what we pray is that everyone will see the "son shining through us." We strive to glorify God and represent him in everything we do to ultimately give God the glory. Our very life is an opportunity to spread the love of Jesus and to let others know where our joy comes from. It comes from our faith and belief in God. I learned this from my mother.

A Woman of Faith

Our Daily Bread is a daily devotional that I've seen my mom read since I was a child. When I visit her today, you can still find her spending the first few minutes of her day alone with her *Our Daily Bread* devotional, other devotionals, and her Bible. My father often worked a late shift during the weekdays and sometimes on the weekends so it was my mom who took us to church. We'd learn to say grace before eating dinner, our prayers at bedtime, and Mom would remind of us how God had blessed her and our family. It was God that gave her a grandmother that introduced her to God and the strength to care for her younger siblings and cousin at a young age. It was God that blessed her with her job, children, and grandchildren and allowed her to see over 51 years of marriage. My mom remembers learning the Model Prayer or Our Father's Prayer at a young age, which can be found in the Holy Bible in the gospel according to Matthew 6:9-13, and reads, "Our Father in heaven, Hallowed be Your name. Your kingdom come. Your will be done on earth as it is in heaven. Give us this day our daily bread. And forgive us our debts, As we forgive our debtors. And do not lead us into temptation, But deliver us from the evil one. For Yours is the kingdom and the power and the glory forever. Amen."[3] I too have developed a personal relationship with Jesus Christ that began with a foundation of attending church and participating in church programs and fellowshipping with other believers all orchestrated by Mom. My faith and spiritual strength were shaped by the example that my mom set. I too start my day reading the *Our Daily Bread* devotionals and scriptures but instead of relying on the small pamphlets I saw my mom read, I access it from an app on my phone.

A Warm Smile and a Positive Attitude

A few of my friends and co-workers call me "Sunshine." They say it's because of how I light up the room when I enter. I think it's my smile and hopefully my energy. This too, comes from my mom. My mom says we should always smile. She says that you'll feel better if you just put a smile on your face. You know what, she's right. I believe

---

[3] New King James Version

that my mother's faith in God allows her to think positively and smile even when she's hurting. In the summer of 1997, my parents were on a cruise with friends and their dream home was struck by lightning and caught on fire. The home and all of its contents were destroyed. The home built by family members on the land once owned by my grandparents was now gone. My grandfather, Jimmy Turner, thought it would be a good investment and for years my grandmother, Annabell, received income from selling the timber on the land long after my grandfather had passed away. My parents were the first to build on the land and create a place to call home. We decided since there was nothing they could do while on vacation that we'd wait until they returned home. I recall feeling overwhelmed as my brother, husband, and I met my parents at the airport to deliver the sad news. This was one time that I was glad not to be the eldest child. I wondered how they would react to this news that they'd lost all of their worldly possessions other than the items they had carried on their trip. They asked, "Is everyone okay?" For it wouldn't have been unusual for family to be at their house to check on it. "Yes," we replied. We repeated what the fire marshal told us; the lightning struck the top of the house and the insulation caught fire and spread rapidly throughout the house. He said if anyone had been home, they likely wouldn't have survived. My mom then says, "See, our Father in heaven is a good God. He had us on the water to protect us from the fire." That's my mama, a woman of faith, who always smiles and has a positive attitude. I hope that she knows that her grandmother and mother would be so proud of what she's accomplished in life, but more importantly of whom she has become. In the words of Uncle Eddie, "You done good," mom.

Often when we're saying goodbye to get off a phone call, I'll say, "I love you" and mom's reply is, "I love you more, but you know that." She's right; I know that she loves me.

My brother's family: Aun've, Antoine, Jr., Bernadette and Antoine; my dad, Herbert; maternal grandmother, Annabell Turner; my mom, Margaret and my family; Jaela, Jessica, Sharif, and Dietrich

My mom, Margaret and my dad, Herbert

Made in the USA
Columbia, SC
08 June 2018